Word 2007:
Intermediate

Student Manual

Word 2007: Intermediate

Series Product Managers:	Charles G. Blum and Adam A. Wilcox
Writer:	Chris Hale
Developmental Editor:	Leslie Garrison
Copyeditor:	Catherine Oliver
Keytester:	Cliff Coryea
Series Designer:	Adam A. Wilcox

Trademarks

ILT Series is a trademark of Axzo Press.

Microsoft is a trademark or registered trademark of Microsoft Corporation in the United States and/or other countries.

Some of the product names and company names used in this book have been used for identification purposes only and may be trademarks or registered trademarks of their respective manufacturers and sellers.

Disclaimers

We reserve the right to revise this publication and make changes from time to time in its content without notice.

Axzo Press is independent from Microsoft Corporation, and not affiliated with Microsoft in any manner. While this publication may be used in assisting individuals to prepare for a Microsoft Business Certification exam, Microsoft, its dedicated program administrator, and Axzo Press do not warrant that use of this publication will ensure passing a Microsoft Business Certification exam.

Student Manual
ISBN-10: 1-4239-1834-7
ISBN-13: 978-1-4239-1834-9

Student Manual with data CD and CBT
ISBN-10: 1-4239-1836-3
ISBN-13: 978-1-4239-1836-3

Printed in the United States of America

1 2 3 4 5 6 7 8 9 10 GL 11 10 09

What is the Microsoft Business Certification Program?

The Microsoft Business Certification Program enables candidates to show that they have something exceptional to offer—proven expertise in Microsoft Office programs. The two certification tracks allow candidates to choose how they want to exhibit their skills, either through validating skills within a specific Microsoft product or taking their knowledge to the next level and combining Microsoft programs to show that they can apply multiple skill sets to complete more complex office tasks. Recognized by businesses and schools around the world, over 3 million certifications have been obtained in over 100 different countries. The Microsoft Business Certification Program is the only Microsoft-approved certification program of its kind.

What is the Microsoft Certified Application Specialist Certification?

The Microsoft Certified Application Specialist Certification exams focus on validating specific skill sets within each of the Microsoft® Office system programs. The candidate can choose which exam(s) they want to take according to which skills they want to validate. The available Application Specialist exams include:

- Using Microsoft® Windows Vista™
- Using Microsoft® Office Word 2007
- Using Microsoft® Office Excel® 2007
- Using Microsoft® Office PowerPoint® 2007
- Using Microsoft® Office Access 2007
- Using Microsoft® Office Outlook® 2007

What is the Microsoft Certified Application Professional Certification?

The Microsoft Certified Application Professional Certification exams focus on a candidate's ability to use the 2007 Microsoft® Office system to accomplish industry-agnostic functions, for example Budget Analysis and Forecasting, or Content Management and Collaboration. The available Application Professional exams currently include:

- Organizational Support
- Creating and Managing Presentations
- Content Management and Collaboration
- Budget Analysis and Forecasting

What do the Microsoft Business Certification Vendor of Approved Courseware logos represent?

Microsoft
CERTIFIED
*Application
Specialist*

Approved Courseware

Microsoft
CERTIFIED
*Application
Professional*

Approved Courseware

The logos validate that the courseware has been approved by the Microsoft® Business Certification Vendor program and that these courses cover objectives that will be included in the relevant exam. It also means that after utilizing this courseware, you may be prepared to pass the exams required to become a Microsoft Certified Application Specialist or Microsoft Certified Application Professional.

For more information

To learn more about the Microsoft Certified Application Specialist or Professional exams[1], visit www.microsoft.com/learning/msbc.

To learn about other Microsoft Office Specialist approved courseware from Axzo Press, visit www.axzopress.com.

[1]The availability of Microsoft Certified Application exams varies by Microsoft Office program, program version, and language. Visit www.microsoft.com/learning for exam availability.

Contents

Introduction

After reading this introduction, you will know how to:

A Use ILT Series training manuals in general.

B Use prerequisites, a target student description, course objectives, and a skills inventory to properly set your expectations for the course.

C Re-key this course after class.

Topic A: About the manual

ILT Series philosophy

ILT Series training manuals facilitate your learning by providing structured interaction with the software itself. While we provide text to explain difficult concepts, the hands-on activities are the focus of our courses. By paying close attention as your instructor leads you through these activities, you will learn the skills and concepts effectively.

We believe strongly in the instructor-led class. During class, focus on your instructor. Our manuals are designed and written to facilitate your interaction with your instructor, and not to call attention to manuals themselves.

We believe in the basic approach of setting expectations, delivering instruction, and providing summary and review afterwards. For this reason, lessons begin with objectives and end with summaries. We also provide overall course objectives and a course summary to provide both an introduction to and closure on the entire course.

Manual components

The manuals contain these major components:

- Table of contents
- Introduction
- Units
- Course summary
- Quick reference
- Glossary
- Index

Each element is described below.

Table of contents

The table of contents acts as a learning roadmap.

Introduction

The introduction contains information about our training philosophy and our manual components, features, and conventions. It contains target student, prerequisite, objective, and setup information for the specific course.

Units

Units are the largest structural component of the course content. A unit begins with a title page that lists objectives for each major subdivision, or topic, within the unit. Within each topic, conceptual and explanatory information alternates with hands-on activities. Units conclude with a summary comprising one paragraph for each topic, and an independent practice activity that gives you an opportunity to practice the skills you've learned.

The conceptual information takes the form of text paragraphs, exhibits, lists, and tables. The activities are structured in two columns, one telling you what to do, the other providing explanations, descriptions, and graphics.

Course summary

This section provides a text summary of the entire course. It is useful for providing closure at the end of the course. The course summary also indicates the next course in this series, if there is one, and lists additional resources you might find useful as you continue to learn about the software.

Quick reference

The quick reference is an at-a-glance job aid summarizing some of the more common features of the software.

Glossary

The glossary provides definitions for all of the key terms used in this course.

Index

The index at the end of this manual makes it easy for you to find information about a particular software component, feature, or concept.

Manual conventions

We've tried to keep the number of elements and the types of formatting to a minimum in the manuals. This aids in clarity and makes the manuals more classically elegant looking. But there are some conventions and icons you should know about.

Item	Description
Italic text	In conceptual text, indicates a new term or feature.
Bold text	In unit summaries, indicates a key term or concept. In an independent practice activity, indicates an explicit item that you select, choose, or type.
`Code font`	Indicates code or syntax.
`Longer strings of ▶` `code will look ▶` `like this.`	In the hands-on activities, any code that's too long to fit on a single line is divided into segments by one or more continuation characters (▶). This code should be entered as a continuous string of text.
Select **bold item**	In the left column of hands-on activities, bold sans-serif text indicates an explicit item that you select, choose, or type.
Keycaps like (↵ ENTER)	Indicate a key on the keyboard you must press.

Hands-on activities

The hands-on activities are the most important parts of our manuals. They are divided into two primary columns. The "Here's how" column gives short instructions to you about what to do. The "Here's why" column provides explanations, graphics, and clarifications. Here's a sample:

Do it!

A-1:   Creating a commission formula

Here's how	Here's why
1 Open Sales	This is an oversimplified sales compensation worksheet. It shows sales totals, commissions, and incentives for five sales reps.
2 Observe the contents of cell F4	F4 ▼ = =E4*C_Rate The commission rate formulas use the name "C_Rate" instead of a value for the commission rate.

For these activities, we have provided a collection of data files designed to help you learn each skill in a real-world business context. As you work through the activities, you will modify and update these files. Of course, you might make a mistake and therefore want to re-key the activity starting from scratch. To make it easy to start over, you will rename each data file at the end of the first activity in which the file is modified. Our convention for renaming files is to add the word "My" to the beginning of the file name. In the above activity, for example, a file called "Sales" is being used for the first time. At the end of this activity, you would save the file as "My sales," thus leaving the "Sales" file unchanged. If you make a mistake, you can start over using the original "Sales" file.

In some activities, however, it might not be practical to rename the data file. If you want to retry one of these activities, ask your instructor for a fresh copy of the original data file.

Topic B: Setting your expectations

Properly setting your expectations is essential to your success. This topic will help you do that by providing:

- Prerequisites for this course
- A description of the target student
- A list of the objectives for the course
- A skills assessment for the course

Course prerequisites

Before taking this course, you should be familiar with personal computers and the use of a keyboard and a mouse. Furthermore, this course assumes that you've completed the following courses or have equivalent experience:

- *Windows XP: Basic*
- *Word 2007: Basic*

Target student

The target student for this course has some experience with Word 2007 and wants to learn how to work with styles, work with sections and columns, format tables, print labels and envelopes, work with graphics, use templates, manage document revisions, and use Web features.

Microsoft Certified Application Specialist certification

This course is designed to help you pass the Microsoft Certified Application Specialist exam for Word 2007. For comprehensive certification training, you should complete all of the following courses:

- *Word 2007: Basic*
- *Word 2007: Intermediate*
- *Word 2007: Advanced*

Course objectives

These overall course objectives will give you an idea about what to expect from the course. It is also possible that they will help you see that this course is not the right one for you. If you think you either lack the prerequisite knowledge or already know most of the subject matter to be covered, you should let your instructor know that you think you are misplaced in the class.

Note: In addition to the general objectives listed below, specific Microsoft Certified Application Specialist exam objectives are listed at the beginning of each topic (where applicable). To download a complete mapping of exam objectives to ILT Series content, go to: www.virtualrom.com/177E36353

After completing this course, you will know how to:

- Examine text formatting and compare the formatting of two selections; apply and create paragraph and character styles; modify and override styles; import and export styles; create, organize, and format a document outline; and use the Document Map and thumbnails.

- Create and format sections of text by using section breaks, headers and footers, and page numbering; and format text into columns.

- Align text in a table; merge and split cells; change text orientation; resize rows; change table borders and cell shading; sort data; split a table; repeat a header row on multiple pages; enter a formula; and apply and modify table styles.

- Prepare and print a label and an envelope.

- Create a document from a template; save and use your own template; store a custom template; use the Building Blocks Organizer to work with commonly used document elements; protect a document with a password; and view and edit document properties.

- Create and modify a diagram; insert and modify text boxes and shapes; and use WordArt, drop caps, and pull quotes to graphically format text.

- Track changes while editing; review and accept revisions; view changes by different reviewers; restrict edits to tracked changes; merge revisions; and insert, print, and delete comments.

- Preview a document as a Web page; save a document as a Web page; open an HTML document in a browser; edit an HTML document in Word; and use hyperlinks in a document.

Skills inventory

Use the following form to gauge your skill level entering the class. For each skill listed, rate your familiarity from 1 to 5, with 5 being the most familiar. *This is not a test.* Rather, it is intended to provide you with an idea of where you're starting from at the beginning of class. If you're wholly unfamiliar with all the skills, you might not be ready for the class. If you think you already understand all of the skills, you might need to move on to the next course in the series. In either case, you should let your instructor know as soon as possible.

Skill	1	2	3	4	5
Using the Reveal Formatting pane					
Applying styles					
Creating a style by example					
Basing one style on another					
Modifying styles					
Overriding styles					
Importing and exporting styles					
Creating, organizing, and formatting outlines					
Using the Document Map pane and the Thumbnails pane					
Inserting section breaks					
Formatting sections					
Inserting section headers and footers					
Formatting section page numbers					
Formatting text into columns and inserting column breaks					
Aligning text in table cells					
Merging and splitting table cells					
Changing row height in a table					
Changing table borders and shading table cells					
Sorting table data					
Splitting a table					
Repeating the header row					
Entering a formula in a table					

Skill	1	2	3	4	5
Applying and modifying table styles					
Printing labels and envelopes					
Creating and formatting organization charts					
Drawing and editing shapes					
Inserting and formatting text boxes					
Arranging multiple objects					
Changing shapes					
Inserting and modifying WordArt					
Using templates					
Protecting access to a document					
Viewing and editing document properties					
Viewing document statistics					
Tracking changes in a document					
Merging revisions from two documents into one					
Working with comments					
Using Web features					
Inserting and navigating with hyperlinks					

Topic C: Re-keying the course

If you have the proper hardware and software, you can re-key this course after class. This section explains what you'll need in order to do so, and how to do it.

Hardware requirements

Your personal computer should have:

- A keyboard and a mouse
- Pentium 500 MHz processor (or higher)
- 256 MB RAM (or higher)
- 4 GB of available hard drive space
- CD-ROM drive
- SVGA at 1024×768, or higher resolution monitor

Software requirements

You will also need the following software:

- Windows XP, Windows Vista, or Windows Server 2003
- Microsoft Office 2007

Network requirements

The following network components and connectivity are also required for rekeying this course:

- Internet access, for the following purposes:
  - Updating the Windows operating system and Microsoft Office 2007 at update.microsoft.com
  - Downloading the Student Data files (if necessary)
  - Downloading document templates from Microsoft Office Online (If online templates are not available, you will not be able to complete activities A-1 and A-2 in the unit titled "Templates and building blocks.")

Setup instructions to re-key the course

Before you re-key the course, you will need to perform the following steps.

1   Open Internet Explorer and navigate to update.microsoft.com. Update the operating system with the latest critical updates and service packs.

2   If your operating system is Windows XP, then launch the Control Panel, open the Display Properties dialog box, and apply the following settings:

   • Theme — Windows XP

   • Screen resolution — 1024 by 768 pixels

   • Color quality — High (24 bit) or higher

   If you choose not to apply these display settings, your screen might not match the screen shots in this manual.

3   If Windows was already loaded on this PC, verify that Internet Explorer is the default Web browser. (If you installed Windows yourself, skip this step.)

   a   Click Start and choose All Programs, Internet Explorer.

   b   Choose Tools, Internet Options.

   c   On the Properties tab, check "Internet Explorer should check to see whether it is the default browser."

   d   Click OK to close the Internet Options dialog box.

   e   Close and re-open Internet Explorer.

   f   If a prompt appears, asking you to make Internet Explorer your default browser, click Yes.

   g   Close Internet Explorer.

4   If necessary, reset any Microsoft Word 2007 defaults that you have changed. If you do not wish to reset the defaults, you can still re-key the course, but some activities might not work exactly as documented. For example, if the Quick Access toolbar displays any custom buttons, then reset it. (Click the down-arrow on its right edge, choose Customize Quick Access Toolbar, click Reset toolbar, and click OK.)

5   Create a folder named Student Data at the root of the hard drive. For a standard hard drive setup, this will be C:\Student Data.

6   Download the student data files for the course. (If you do not have an Internet connection, you can ask your instructor for a copy of the data files on a disk.)

   a   Connect to www.courseilt.com/instructor_tools.html.

   b   Click the link for Microsoft Word 2007 to display a page of course listings, and then click the link for Word 2007: Intermediate.

   c   Click the link for downloading the student data files, and follow the instructions that appear on your screen.

7   Copy the data files to the Student Data folder.

8   To ensure that you won't get a security warning when you open files in Word, designate the Student Data folder as a Trusted Location:

    a   Click the Office button and choose Word Options to open the Word Options dialog box.

    b   On the Trust Center page, click Trust Center Settings to open the Trust Center dialog box.

    c   Navigate to the Trusted Locations page.

    d   Click Add new location. The Microsoft Office 2007 Trusted Location dialog box opens.

    e   Click Browse and navigate to the Student Data folder.

    f   Click OK to close the Browse dialog box.

    g   Check "Subfolders of this location are also trusted."

    h   Click OK to close the Microsoft Office 2007 Trusted Location dialog box.

    i   Click OK to close the Trust Center dialog box.

    j   Click OK to close the Word Options dialog box.

    k   Close Word.

9   If necessary, change the folder options in Windows Explorer so that hidden files and folders are shown.

    a   Open Windows Explorer.

    b   Choose Tools, Folder Options and activate the View tab.

    c   Under Advanced settings, select "Show hidden files and folders."

    d   Click OK to close the Folder Options dialog box.

You will not be able to complete activity A-4 in the unit titled "Templates and building blocks" unless hidden files and folders are shown.

CertBlaster exam preparation software

If you plan to take the Microsoft Certified Application Specialist exam for Word 2007, we encourage you to use the CertBlaster pre- and post-assessment software that comes with this course. To download and install your free software:

1   Go to www.courseilt.com/certblaster.

2   Click the link for Word 2007.

3   Save the .EXE file to a folder on your hard drive. (Note: If you skip this step, the CertBlaster software will not install correctly.)

4   Click Start and choose Run.

5   Click Browse and then navigate to the folder that contains the .EXE file.

6   Select the .EXE file and click Open.

7   Click OK and follow the on-screen instructions. When prompted for the password, enter **c_601**.

Unit 1
Styles

Unit time: 75 minutes

Complete this unit, and you'll know how to:

A Examine and compare text formatting by using the Reveal Formatting task pane.

B Apply and create paragraph and character styles.

C Modify, override, and export styles.

D Create, organize, and format a document outline.

E View a document by using the Document Map and thumbnails.

Topic A: Examining formatting

This topic covers the following Microsoft Certified Application Specialist exam objective for Word 2007.

#	Objective
2.1.2	**Create and modify styles**
	• Reveal style formatting

The Reveal Formatting task pane

Explanation

You can tell what formatting you've applied to text by examining the Font and Paragraph dialog boxes. But a faster way to see all of the formatting applied to a selection is to use the Reveal Formatting task pane. In addition, you can compare the formatting of two selections.

Viewing formatting

The Reveal Formatting pane displays the font and paragraph formatting of the selected text. To open the Reveal Formatting pane, press Shift+F1.

Select some text to view its formatting information. For example, in Exhibit 1-1, the heading "Contents" appears in the Selected text box. The applied formatting is displayed under "Formatting of selected text." Exhibit 1-1 shows that the heading's font format is Trebuchet MS, 26 pt, bold, and has the color Accent 2 applied to it. You can click Font (the blue underlined text) to open the Font dialog box and change the formatting.

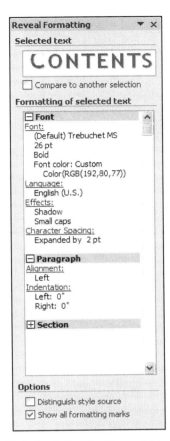

Exhibit 1-1: The Reveal Formatting pane

Comparing formatting

You also can use the Reveal Formatting pane to compare the text formatting of two selections. To do so, verify that the first selection appears in the Selected text box. Then check "Compare to another selection" to display a second Selected text box. Finally, select the text to be compared. The result of the comparison is shown in the Formatting differences box.

A-1:   Using the Reveal Formatting pane

Here's how	Here's why
1 Start Word	Click Start and choose All Programs, Microsoft Office, Microsoft Office Word 2007.
Maximize the window	If necessary.
2 Open Spice info	From the current unit folder.
Save the document as **My spice info**	In the current unit folder.
3 Show the hidden formatting symbols	In the Paragraph group, click the Show/Hide button.
4 Move to page 2	The Contents page
5 Select the heading **Contents**	
6 Press (SHIFT) + (F1)	To open the Reveal Formatting pane, which displays the formatting of the selected text.
7 In the Reveal Formatting pane, click **Font**, as shown	⊟ **Font** Font: (Default) Trebuchet MS 26 pt Bold To open the Font dialog box.
From the Size list, select **24**	
Clear **Shadow**	
Click **OK**	To close the dialog box and apply the formatting. The Reveal Formatting pane is updated to reflect the format changes.
8 In the Reveal Formatting pane, check **Compare to another selection**	You'll compare the "Contents" heading with the heading on page 3.

9 Scroll to page 3	By using the scrollbar, you ensure that "Contents" remains selected.
Select the heading **The long history of spices**	This heading's formatting is different from that of the other heading. You'll observe the differences in formatting and then set the formatting to match.
Observe the Formatting differences box	

> ⊟ **Font**
> Font:
>   24 pt -> 26 pt
> Effects:
>   Not Shadow -> Shadow

The differences in the two sections of text appear in the box. The first selection has a font size of 24 pt; the second selection has a font size of 26 pt. In addition, the first selection does not use the shadow effect, and the second does.

10 In the Font group, from the Font Size list, select **24**	To reduce the font size to 24 pt.
Observe the Formatting differences box	Now only the Effects are different.
11 Remove the shadow effect from the heading on page 3	(Use the Font dialog box; open it by clicking Effects in the Reveal Formatting pane.) The Reveal Formatting pane indicates that there are no more formatting differences.
12 Close the Reveal Formatting pane	
13 Update the document	

Topic B: Creating styles

This topic covers the following Microsoft Certified Application Specialist exam objectives for Word 2007.

#	Objective
1.1.2	**Apply Quick Styles to documents**
2.1.1	**Apply styles**
	• Change from one style to another (This objective is also covered in *Word 2007: Basic*, in the unit titled "Proofing and printing documents.")
	• Format headings
2.1.2	**Create and modify styles**
	• Create new styles
	• Change fonts
	• Create new style based on existing styles
2.1.3	**Format characters**
	• Clear formatting (This objective is also covered in *Word 2007: Basic*, in the unit titled "Formatting text.")

Applying styles

Explanation

A *style* is a named set of formatting options (font, font size, font color, effects, and so on) that define the appearance of recurring text elements, such as headings or body text. By using a style, you can apply several formats in one step. For example, if you want all of the section titles in a document to be 16-point Cambria, you can apply the Heading 2 style to them. Styles can help you maintain formatting consistency within and among documents.

You can apply a style to selected text by activating the Home tab and selecting the desired style from the Styles gallery, shown in Exhibit 1-2. If you don't like the style that's applied, you can select another option from the gallery, which is accessible from the Styles group.

Word provides several built-in styles. For example, you can apply the Heading 1 style to format selected text as a heading. By default, when you create a document, Word applies the Normal style to the entire document.

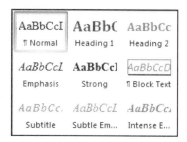

Exhibit 1-2: The gallery of styles

Quick Styles

A *Quick Style* is a set of styles that complement each other. By selecting a single Quick Style, you can format document text easily to create an attractive, professional, and cohesive appearance. To apply a Quick Style set to a document:

1 On the Home tab, in the Styles group, click Change Styles.

2 Choose Style Set to display a list of available Quick Styles.

3 Select the desired Quick Style set.

Do it!

B-1:   Applying a style

Here's how	Here's why
1 Click in the line **The long history of spices**	(Located at the top of page 3.) You don't have to select the entire heading.
2 In the Styles group, click **Heading 1**	To apply the Heading 1 style to the page heading. This style formats the text as blue, bold, 16pt Cambria.
3 Click in the line **Introduction**	You'll apply a style to this text.
4 In the Styles group, click as shown	AaBbCcl Heading 3
	(The More button.) To display additional styles.
In the gallery, point to different styles	To preview the appearance of various styles. Notice how each style applies a set of formats to the selected text, "Introduction."
5 In the gallery, select **Heading 2**	To apply the Heading 2 style to the subheading.
6 In the Styles group, click **Change Styles**	
Choose **Style Set**	To display a list of Quick Style sets.
7 Point to each of the Quick Style sets	Notice how each set formats all of the text. Each Quick Style set contains complementary styles for body text and several heading levels.
Click **Change Styles**	To close the list and return to the document.
8 Update the document	

Creating styles by example

Explanation

You might have formatted some text by using a combination of options that you want to apply to other text. If you plan to use the same combination of formats repeatedly, you can create a new style based on the formatting of selected text.

To create a style based on selected text:

1 Select the text on which you want to base the new style.

2 In the Styles group, click the Dialog Box Launcher to open the Styles task pane, shown in Exhibit 1-3.

3 In the Styles task pane, click the New Style button to open the Create New Style from Formatting dialog box, shown in Exhibit 1-4.

4 Enter a name for the new style.

5 Press Enter to use the selected formats and to create the style, which will now be available in the Styles gallery and the Styles list.

You can clear all the formatting from selected text by clicking the Clear Formatting button in the Font group.

The Styles pane

You can use the Styles pane to create, modify, and apply styles. You can either create a style from scratch or modify an existing style and save it with a new name.

To apply a style by using the Styles pane, first select the text to which you want to apply a style. Then, from the Styles list, select the desired style.

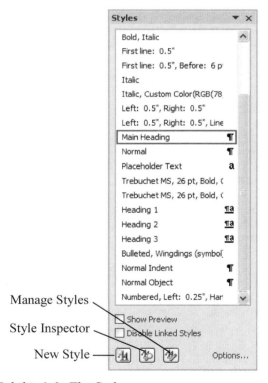

Exhibit 1-3: The Styles pane

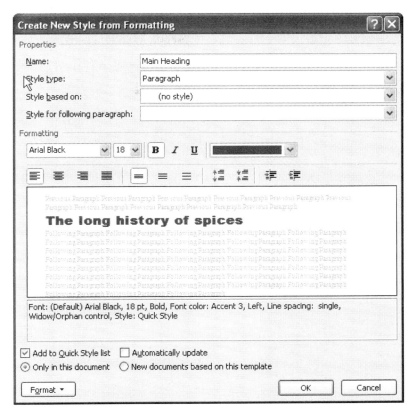

Exhibit 1-4: The Create New Style from Formatting dialog box

B-2: Creating a style by example

Here's how	Here's why
1 Select the entire line containing **The long history of spices**	
In the Font group, click [image]	(The Clear Formatting button.) To clear the formatting from the selected text.
Format the text as Arial Black, bold, 18 point, dark olive green	Use the options in the Font group. Select the Olive Green, Accent 3, Darker 50% color.
2 Click as shown	
	To open the Styles pane.
Click [image]	(The New Style button.) To open the Create New Style from Formatting dialog box.
Edit the Name box to read **Main Heading**	
From the Style based on list, select **(no style)**	So that the new style does not inherit any style attributes from another style.
Click **OK**	To create the style. It now appears in both the Styles pane, as shown in Exhibit 1-3, and the Styles group.
	You'll now apply it to the other main headings in the document.
3 At the top of page 2, place the insertion point in the heading **Contents**	
In the Styles group, click **Main Heading**	To apply the Main Heading style to the text.
4 Update the document	

Basing styles on other styles

Another way to create a style is to base it on an existing style. The new style will inherit the formatting of the style it's based on, and any additional formats you select will either replace or be added to the inherited options. For example, suppose you create a section-heading style named "Appendix Heading." You want this style to have the same formatting as the Heading 1 style, but you want the text to be red. Rather than manually repeating the formatting of Heading 1, you can base the new style on it and then specify the red font color for the new style.

To base one style on another:

1 In the Styles pane, click the New Style button.
2 Enter a name for the new style.
3 From the Style based on list, select the style you want to base the new one on.
4 Under Formatting, select any other formatting options you want to apply to the new style. Any formats you select will override the formatting from the "parent" style.
5 Click OK.

B-3:   Basing one style on another

Here's how	Here's why
1 On page 3, place the insertion point in the text **Introduction**	
In the Styles pane, click **Clear All**	(At the top of the Styles list.) To clear the formatting from the text.
In the Styles pane, click [icon]	To open the Create New Style from Formatting dialog box.
2 Edit the Name box to read **Subheading 1**	
From the Style based on list, select **Main Heading**	This time, you do want the style to use another style's formats, plus those that you change.
3 From the Font Size list, select **14**	
From the Font Color list, select the dark red color, as shown	

Red, Accent 2, Darker 50%.

4 Click **OK**	To create the style and apply it to "Introduction."
5 At the top of page 4, place the insertion point within **The medicinal use of spices**	
In the Styles pane, select **Subheading 1**	
On page 5, apply the Subheading 1 style to **The spice trade**	
6 On page 4, place the insertion point within **Spices as ancient medicine**	
Open the Create New style from Formatting dialog box	In the Styles pane, click the New Style button.
7 Name the style **Subheading 2**	
Base this style on Subheading 1	The new style will inherit formatting from Subheading 1, which, in turn, inherits formatting from Main Heading.
Format the font size as 12 point	The new style will also use the italics and underlining that are already applied to the text.
Click **OK**	
8 Apply the Subheading 2 style to **Spices as modern medicine**	(Located farther down on page 4.) Click in the text and select Subheading 2 from the Styles pane.
On page 5, apply the Subheading 2 style to **A funny thing happened on the way to the Spice Lands...**	
9 Move to page 6	(This page begins with "Bay leaf.") This page and the next six pages have similar headings and subheadings.
Apply the Subheading 2 style to **About this spice**, **How to use this spice**, and **Spice trivia** for each spice page	Pages 6 through 12.
10 Update the document	

More formatting options for styles

Explanation

In addition to font formats, you can include other formatting options in a style. For example, you can use styles to apply paragraph, tab, and border formatting to text.

To select additional formatting options for a new style:

1 In the Create New Style from Formatting dialog box, click Format to show the additional formatting options.

2 Select the kind of formatting you want to change. The corresponding dialog box will open.

3 Set the desired options, and then click OK to close the dialog box.

4 Click OK to save the settings and close the Create New Style from Formatting dialog box.

Do it!

B-4: Controlling pagination by using styles

Here's how	Here's why
1 Move to page 6	You will define a style for spice names that also includes pagination control.
Place the insertion point in the heading **Bay leaf**	At the top of the page.
2 Open the Create New Style from Formatting dialog box	In the Styles pane, click the New Style button.
3 Name the style **Spice Name**	
Format the text as Trebuchet MS, 14 point, bold	
Click **Format**	To display the Format menu.
Choose **Paragraph...**	To open the Paragraph dialog box.
4 Activate the Line and Page Breaks tab	
Check **Page break before**	
Click **OK**	To close the Paragraph dialog box.
Click **OK**	To close the Create New Style from Formatting dialog box. Because there was already a page break before the spice name on this page, there is now an extra one.

5 Move to page 6	It's blank, except for the page-break symbol.
Select the page break	Click it.
Press (DELETE)	To delete the manual page break. The page break included with the style does not appear as a formatting symbol in the document.
At the bottom of page 6, apply the **Spice Name** style to **Cinnamon**	Observe that the page breaks above the spice name.
Apply the **Spice Name** style to the remaining spice names	Cloves, Coriander, Cumin, Nutmeg, Pepper, Star anise, and Turmeric.
6 Update the document	

Character styles

Explanation The default style type for creating a style is paragraph, but you can also create character styles. A character style is similar to a paragraph style, except that a character style applies to only the selected text, as shown in Exhibit 1-5, and it does not include paragraph formats. (A paragraph style can include both character and paragraph formats, and it applies to all text in a paragraph.) You can use a character style to format specific text without affecting the formatting of the other text in the paragraph.

To create a character style:

1 Open the Create New Style from Formatting dialog box.
2 Name the style.
3 From the Style type list, select Character.
4 Select the desired formatting options.
5 Click OK.

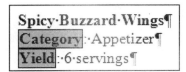

Exhibit 1-5: Text using a character style (the words "Category" and "Yield")

Do it!   **B-5: Creating a character style**

Here's how	Here's why
1 On page 16, select **Category**	Below the text "Spicy Buzzard Wings."
2 Open the Create New Style from Formatting dialog box	In the Styles pane, click the New Style button.
Name the style **Label**	
From the Style type list, select **Character**	So that the style's formatting will be applied to selected characters, rather than to entire paragraphs.
Format the text as bold and dark red	
3 Click **Format** and choose **Border...**	To open the Borders and Shading dialog box.
Under Setting, click as shown	
	To apply a border to all four sides of the text.
Activate the Shading tab	
From the Fill list, select the Olive Green, Accent 3 color	
4 Click **OK**	To close the Borders and Shading dialog box.
Click **OK**	To close the Create New Style from Formatting dialog box.
5 Select the word **Yield**	Under "Spicy Buzzard Wings."
In the Styles pane, select **Label**	
6 Apply the **Label** style to the **Category** and **Yield** labels for each recipe	
7 Update the document	

Topic C: Modifying styles

This topic covers the following Microsoft Certified Application Specialist exam objectives for Word 2007.

#	Objective
2.1.1	**Apply styles**
	• Format body text
2.1.3	**Format characters**
	• Change font case

Managing styles

Explanation

One of the advantages of using styles is the ease with which you can make global changes. For example, if you modify any of a style's properties, then all text formatted with that style automatically inherits the new properties. If your document contains multiple headings, subheadings, and other elements to which you've applied styles, you can see that this feature can be a big time-saver.

To modify a style, use the Modify Style dialog box. To open the Modify Style dialog box, do either of the following:

- In the Styles pane, point to the name of the style you want to modify. Click the down-arrow to the right of the style name, and choose Modify.

- In the Styles pane, click the Manage Styles button to open the Manage Styles dialog box, shown in Exhibit 1-6. Select the name of the style you want to modify, and click Modify.

In the Modify Style dialog box, you can adjust the style's formatting just as you did in the Create New Style from Formatting dialog box.

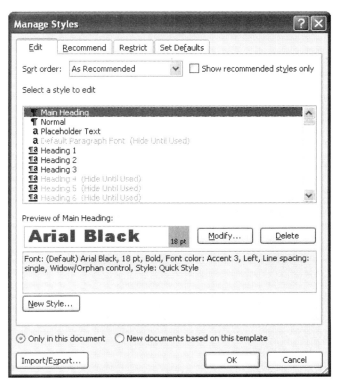

Exhibit 1-6: The Manage Styles dialog box

Automatically updating styles

You can have Word update a style automatically every time you apply manual formatting to text with that style applied. To do so, open the Modify Style dialog box for that style and check Automatically update.

Do it!

C-1: Modifying a style

Here's how	Here's why
1 Scroll through the document	To observe that text with the Main Heading, Subheading 1, and Subheading 2 styles all use the font Arial Black. You'll change the styles so that they all use Trebuchet MS.
2 In the Styles pane, click [icon]	(The Manage Styles button.) To open the Manage Styles dialog box.
3 From the "Select a style to edit" list, select **Main Heading**	You might need to scroll to the top of the list.
Click **Modify**	To open the Modify Style dialog box.
4 From the Font list, select **Trebuchet MS**	
Click **OK**	To return to the Manage Styles dialog box.
Click **OK**	To close the dialog box.
5 Observe the text on pages 3 and 4	The Main Heading, Subheading 1, and Subheading 2 styles now use the Trebuchet MS font, because Subheading 1 is based on Main Heading, and Subheading 2 is based on Subheading 1.
6 Update the document	

Overriding styles

Explanation

There might be times when you want to change the formatting of text after applying a style to it. For example, after applying the Heading 1 style, you might decide to increase the heading font to 20pt and change the case to small capital letters. You do this by selecting the text and applying the desired formatting. This action overrides the formatting contained in the style locally, without affecting the style's formatting options globally.

When you override a style, the Styles pane shows it as a new style, with the additional formatting next to the style name, as shown in Exhibit 1-7.

Note: The automatic-update feature controls whether styles can be overridden. If you check Automatically update when defining a style, then any formatting you add in the document will modify the style's global definition, rather than overriding the formatting locally.

Exhibit 1-7: The Main Heading style, showing that the selected text overrides the style formatting

Deleting styles

You can delete a style from a document by using the Styles pane. To do so, point to the name of the style you want to delete, click the down-arrow to the right of the style name, and choose Delete. You will be prompted to confirm the deletion. When you delete a paragraph style, text that has been formatted with that style will revert to the Normal paragraph style.

Do it!

C-2: Overriding a style

Here's how	Here's why
1 On page 2, select **Contents**	You've applied the Main Heading style to this text, but you want to change its formatting without affecting any other text using the same style. You can override formatting for an occurrence of a style without removing the rest of the style formatting or affecting other text that uses the style.
2 In the Font group, click the Dialog Box Launcher	To open the Font dialog box.
3 Check **Small caps**	To format the selected text.
4 Activate the Character Spacing tab From the Spacing list, select **Expanded** Click **OK**	 To close the dialog box.
5 Observe the Styles pane	As shown in Exhibit 1-7, a description of the additional formatting appears next to the Main Heading style to indicate that you've overridden it.
6 Update the document	

The Normal style

Explanation

By default, when you create a document, Word applies the Normal style to the entire document. The Normal style uses the default settings for body text in a given document. Any text that you haven't applied a style or manual formatting to uses the Normal style, and Normal is the default "based on" style; therefore, changing the formatting for the Normal style can affect much of the formatting in your document.

Setting style defaults

You can change the default settings for a document by using the Manage Styles dialog box. To do so:

1 In the Styles pane, click the Manage Styles button to open the Manage Styles dialog box.

2 Activate the Set Defaults tab, shown in Exhibit 1-8.

3 Select the desired settings and click OK.

By default, any changes you make in the default settings will be applied to only the current document.

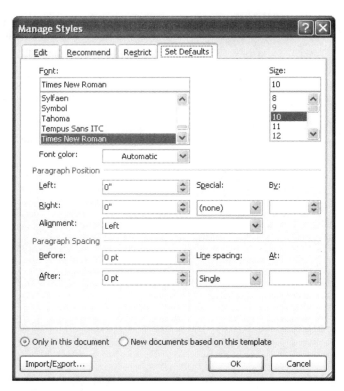

Exhibit 1-8: The Set Defaults tab in the Manage Styles dialog box

Do it!   **C-3:   Modifying the Normal style**

Here's how	Here's why
1 Open the Manage Styles dialog box	In the Styles pane, click the Manage Styles button.
From the "Select a style to edit" list, select **Normal**	
Click **Modify**	To open the Modify Style dialog box.
2 Click **Format** and choose **Paragraph...**	To open the Paragraph dialog box.
Activate the Indents and Spacing tab	
3 Under Indentation, set the Left value to **0.2"**	
Click **OK** three times	To return to the document.
4 On page 3, observe the text	The body text has the new indent settings. So does the text that uses the Spice Name style, because it was based on the Normal style. The other styles, not based on Normal, have their original indent settings.
5 Update the document	

Importing and exporting styles

Explanation

You can import styles from another document and export them from the current document. To import or export styles, follow these steps:

1 In the Manage Styles dialog box, click Import/Export to open the Organizer dialog box, shown in Exhibit 1-9. The styles available in the current document appear in the box on the left; by default, the styles in the Normal template appear on the right.

2 To import styles from or export styles to another document, click the Close File button on the right side of the dialog box; then click Open File.

3 Navigate to the folder containing the document whose styles you want to use.

4 From the Files of type list, select Word Documents.

5 Select the desired document and click Open.

6 Copy styles from one document or the other by selecting the appropriate style from the list and clicking Copy.

7 When you've finished copying styles, click Close.

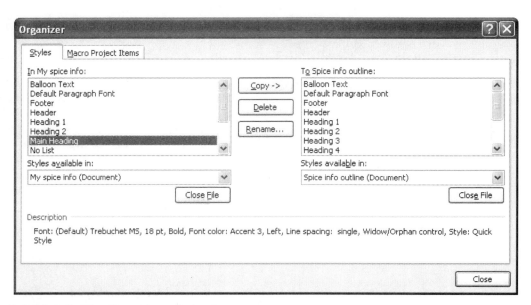

Exhibit 1-9: The Organizer dialog box

Do it!   ### C-4:   Exporting a style

Here's how	Here's why
1 Open the Manage Styles dialog box	You'll export a style from this document so that you can use it in another document.
2 Click **Import/Export**	To open the Organizer dialog box.
On the right side of the dialog box, click **Close File**	To close the Normal template. After you do this, the button changes to Open File.
Click **Open File**	To open the Open dialog box.
3 Navigate to the current unit folder	
From the Files of type list, select **Word Documents**	
Select **Spice info outline**	
Click **Open**	The right-hand list in the Organizer dialog box displays the styles available in Spice info online.
4 From the "In My spice info" list, select **Main Heading**	The list on the left.
5 Click Copy ->	To copy the Main Heading style from the current document to Spice info outline.
6 Click **Close**	To close the dialog box.
Click **No**	(If necessary.) You don't want to save changes at this time.
Update and close all documents	

Topic D: Outlining

Explanation

An outline provides a helpful way to view the main sections of a document. In Word, an outline consists of headings and subheadings that are formatted with an outline level. *Outline view* also helps you with navigating in long documents, because it enables you to collapse and expand text to view different levels.

Using styles to create an outline

When you format a document with Word's predefined heading or subheading styles, Word automatically creates an outline. You can switch to Outline view by clicking the Outline button in the Document Views group on the Views tab or by clicking the Outline button on the status bar.

When you switch to this view, the Outlining tab becomes available on the Ribbon. This tab has three groups: Outline Tools, Master Document, and Close.

To create an outline, you can apply the styles Heading 1, Heading 2, or Heading 3 to text to create Level 1, Level 2, and Level 3 outline levels, as shown in Exhibit 1-10. You can also use the Outline Tools group, shown in Exhibit 1-11, to set and manipulate outline levels.

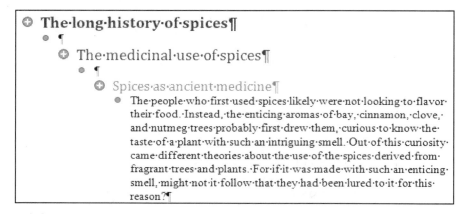

Exhibit 1-10: A document in Outline view, showing Level 1, Level 2, and Level 3 headings

Exhibit 1-11: The Outline Tools group

The following table describes some of the commands available in the Outline Tools group.

Button	Shortcut	Description
↞		Promotes the selected text to the Heading 1 style (Level 1 outline level).
←	ALT + SHIFT + ←	Promotes the selected text to the next highest outline level. If the text is already subordinate to an outline level, that text is promoted to the level to which it is subordinate.
→	ALT + SHIFT + →	Demotes the selected text to the next lowest outline level. If the text already is subordinate to an outline level, it is demoted to the next level below that to which it is subordinate.
↠		Demotes the selected text to the Body text outline level (Normal style).
↑	ALT + SHIFT + ↑	Moves the selected paragraph up in the outline, without changing its outline level.
↓	ALT + SHIFT + ↓	Moves the selected paragraph down in the outline, without changing its outline level.
+	ALT + +	If collapsed, expands the selected outline level.
–	ALT + _	If expanded, collapses the selected outline level.

Do it!

D-1: Creating an outline

Here's how	Here's why
1 Open Spice info outline	From the current unit folder.
	This document doesn't contain any formatting or styles (other than the Normal style). You'll use it to create an outline.
Save the document as **My spice info outline**	In the current unit folder.
2 Open the Styles pane	If necessary.
3 On the status bar, click ▤	(The Outline button.) To view the document as an outline. The Outlining tab appears on the Ribbon and is active.

4 On page 1, place the insertion point within
A word from the chairman

In the Outline Tools group, from
the Outline Level list, select
Level 1

5 On page 2, place the insertion
point within **Contents**

Click    (The Promote to Heading 1 button.) To promote
                                             the text to Level 1 in the outline.

6 On page 3, promote **The long**   Place the insertion point in the text, and click the
history of spices to Level 1   Promote to Heading 1 button.

7 Place the insertion point within
Introduction

Click   (The Demote button.) To demote the text to
                                             Level 2 in the outline.

8 On page 4, observe the text   All of the text after the Level 2 heading that you
                                             just created is subordinate to that heading. Thus,
                                             to set another Level 2 heading, you'll have to
                                             promote the desired text.

Place the insertion point within
The medicinal use of spices

Click   (The Promote button.) To promote the text to
                                             Level 2, one level higher.

9 On page 5, apply the Level 2   Place the insertion point in the text and click the
outline level to   Promote button.
The spice trade

On pages 4 and 5, apply Level 3   Place the insertion point in the text; then click
to the following phrases: the Demote button to set the first level ("Spices
Spices as ancient   as ancient medicine"). Promote the text "Spices
medicine,   as modern medicine" to Level 3. For the third
Spices as modern   subheading, which is already subordinate to a
medicine, and   Level 2 heading, click the Demote button.
A funny thing happened on
the way to the Spice
Lands...

10 Starting on page 6, apply Level 2   Bay leaf, Cinnamon, Cloves, Coriander, Cumin,
to each spice name   Nutmeg, Pepper, Star anise, and Turmeric.

11 Starting on page 12, apply Level 2
to each recipe name

12 Update the document

Organizing outlines

Explanation

You can use Outline view to rearrange an outlined document easily. The plus sign next to an outline level indicates that there is additional text under the level heading, as shown in Exhibit 1-12. Double-click the plus sign to collapse the subordinate text under a level heading, and double-click it again to expand the text.

When you point to a plus sign, the pointer changes to a four-headed arrow, indicating that you can move the outline level. To do so, drag the plus sign to where you want the outline level—as well as any subordinate text—in the outline. For long documents, organizing an outline might be easier with the outline levels collapsed. Alternatively, in the Outline Tools group, click Show First Line Only to show only the first line of each paragraph. Also, you can choose which levels to show by selecting an option from the Show Level list.

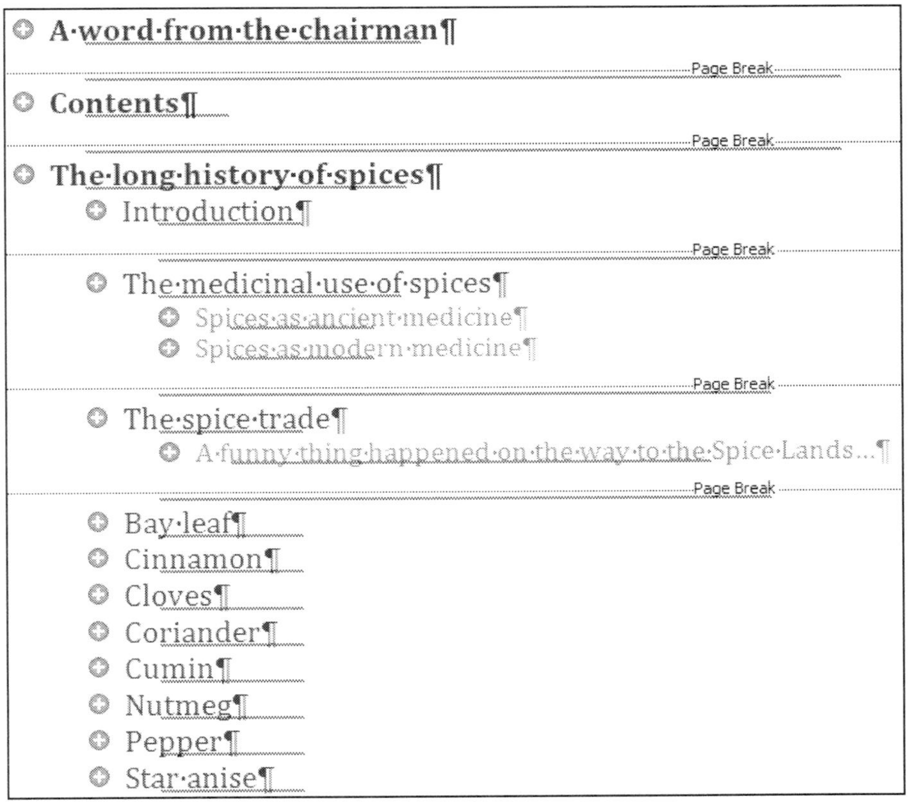

Exhibit 1-12: A document with outline levels collapsed

Do it!

D-2: Organizing an outline

Here's how	Here's why
1 On page 4, double-click the plus sign to the left of "The medicinal use of spices"	To collapse the headings and body text subordinate to that text.
Double-click the plus sign again	To expand the text.
Double-click the plus sign to the left of "Spices as ancient medicine"	Notice that only the text subordinate to that subheading collapses.
Expand the text again	Double-click the plus sign to the left of "Spices as ancient medicine"
2 From the Show Level list, select **Level 3**	(In the Outline Tools group.) To view only Level 1, Level 2, and Level 3 of the outline.
3 Drag the plus sign to the left of "The spice trade" so that it's above "The medicinal use of spices," as shown	In the screen shot below, notice the position of the mouse pointer (the vertical, double-headed arrow). This is the position you're dragging to.

Release the mouse button	To move the subheading "The spice trade" and its subordinate text above the "The medicinal use of spices" subheading.
4 From the Show Level list, select **All Levels**	
5 Update the document	

Formatting text for an outline

Explanation

When you apply an outline level to text in Outline view, Word assigns that text a corresponding style. You can change the formatting for these styles just as you would for a style you created. For example, if you want all Level 1 headings to use the font Trebuchet MS, you can format the Heading 1 style to use that font. To change the formatting for an outline level, select the desired options in the corresponding style's Modify Style dialog box.

Alternatively, you can create a style, specify its outline level, and apply it to text to create an outline. For example, if you had a style named Main Heading, you could specify that it uses outline Level 1. Then, when you apply that style to a heading, it will automatically be formatted as Level 1.

To set the outline level for a style:

1   Open the Modify Style dialog box for the style.

2   Click Format and choose Paragraph.

3   Select an option from the Outline level list.

- For the Normal style, the default level is Body text. Any style based on Normal (the "based on" default) will also use the Body text level for outlining.

- For Heading 1, the default level is Level 1; for Heading 2, it's Level 2; and for Heading 3, it's Level 3.

- There are 10 outline levels: Body text, and Level 1 through Level 9.

4   Click OK.

D-3: Formatting an outline

Here's how	Here's why
1 On the status bar, click ▣	To return to Print Layout view.
Observe the Styles pane	The styles used in the outline (Normal for body text, and Heading 1, Heading 2, and Heading 3) are displayed in the pane.
2 Open the Manage Styles dialog box	Click the Manage Styles button.
Activate the Edit tab	
From the "Select a style to edit" list, select **Heading 1**	
Click **Modify**	To open the Modify Style dialog box.
3 From the Style based on list, select **(no style)**	
Format the style as Trebuchet MS, 18 point, bold, dark green	Use the color Olive Green, Accent 3, Darker 50%.
Click **OK**	To return to the Manage Styles dialog box.
4 Modify the Heading 2 style so that it's based on the Heading 1 style and is Trebuchet MS, 16 point, dark red	Use the color Red, Accent 2, Darker 50%.
5 Modify the Heading 3 style so that it's based on the Heading 1 style and is Trebuchet MS, 14 point, black	
6 From the "Select a style to edit" list, select **Normal**	
Click **Modify**	To open the Modify Style dialog box.
Click **Format** and choose **Paragraph...**	To open the Paragraph dialog box.
7 Under Spacing, in the After box, click the up-arrow	To specify 6 points of space after the paragraph.
Click **OK** three times	To return to the document.
8 Update the document	

Topic E: Using Full Screen Reading view

This topic covers the following Microsoft Certified Application Specialist exam objective for Word 2007.

#	Objective
1.4.1	**Customize Word options** • Disable the open e-mail attachments feature in reading mode

Full Screen Reading view

Explanation

When you want to read a document on screen, you might want to hide the Ribbon and other editing tools so that you can focus on the document's content. To do so, you can click the Full Screen Reading button in the Document Views group on the View tab, or click the Full Screen Reading button in the status bar. In Full Screen Reading mode, you can use the Document Map pane and the Thumbnails pane to navigate in a document.

The Document Map pane

The *Document Map* displays document headings by outline level in a navigational pane—the Document Map pane, shown in Exhibit 1-13. To display this pane when you're using Full Screen Reading view, choose Document Map from the Page menu at the top of the document window.

You can display the Document Map pane in other views, too. On the View tab, in the Show/Hide group, check the Document Map check box.

The Document Map pane can be helpful for navigating through a long document. As you move through the document, corresponding headings on each page are highlighted in the Document Map pane. You can also click the headings in the Document Map pane to go directly to them in the document.

For the Document Map pane to be used, the document must contain heading styles or styles with outline levels defined.

Exhibit 1-13: The Document Map pane

E-1: **Using the Document Map pane**

Here's how	Here's why
1 On the status bar, click 📖	To switch to Full Screen Reading view.
2 Click ▷	(The Next Page button is located above the pages, in the center of the screen.) To move to the next page of the document.
3 From the Page menu, choose **Document Map**	

> Page 5-6 of 17 ▾ ▷
>
> **Jump to a Page**
> 🌐 Go Back ▸
> 🌐 Go Forward ▸
>   Go to Farthest Read Page
>   Go to First Page
>   Go to Last Page
> ➡ Go To...
> 🔍 Find...
> **Jump to a Heading**
>   A word from the chairman (Page 1)
>   Contents (Page 2)
> ✓ The long history of spices (Page 3)
> 🔲 Document Map
> 🔲 Thumbnails

	To display the Document Map pane, which shows an outline of the document.
4 In the Document Map pane, click **Cumin**	To move to that page in the document.

Thumbnails

Explanation

In Word, *thumbnails* are miniature images of the pages in a document. You can use thumbnails to easily navigate through a large document. In Full Screen Reading view, the Thumbnail pane, shown in Exhibit 1-14, appears on the left side of the document window. The page numbers also appear below the thumbnails.

To display thumbnails in Full Screen Reading view, choose Thumbnails from the Page menu. To display thumbnails when you're using Print Layout, Web Layout, Outline, or Draft view, activate the View tab and check Thumbnails in the Show/Hide group.

As you move through the document, the Thumbnails pane updates to show the pages you're viewing. To navigate to a specific page, click its thumbnail image.

Disabling the "open e-mail attachments" feature

When you open an e-mail attachment that's been saved in a Word format, the attachment is displayed in Full Screen Reading view by default. You can disable this feature so that Word e-mail attachments will be opened in Print Layout view instead. To do so, open the Word Options dialog box and verify that Popular is selected in the left pane. In the list of options on the right, clear the "Open e-mail attachments in Full Screen Reading view" option and click OK.

Exhibit 1-14: The Thumbnails pane

E-2: Viewing document thumbnails

Here's how	Here's why
1 From the Switch Navigation Window list, select **Thumbnails**	
	To display the Thumbnails pane.
2 Click the third thumbnail	To move to that page in the document.
3 Click **Close**	(In the upper-right corner of the window.) To return to Print Layout view.
4 Click	
Click **Word Options**	To open the Word Options dialog box.
5 Verify that Popular is selected in the left pane	To display the most popular Word options.
Observe "Open e-mail attachments in Full Screen Reading view"	This option is enabled by default, so Word e-mail attachments will be opened in Full Screen Reading view. If you prefer to open these attachments in Print Layout view instead, you can clear this option and click OK.
Click **Cancel**	To close the Word Options dialog box without making any changes.
6 Update and close the document	

Unit summary: Styles

Topic A   In this topic, you learned how to examine text formatting and compare the formatting of two selections by using the **Reveal Formatting** pane.

Topic B   In this topic, you applied a **style** to some text. Then you learned how to create a style by example and how to base one style on another. Finally, you created a character style.

Topic C   In this topic, you modified a style by using the **Manage Styles** dialog box, and you learned how to override a style. You also learned how to modify the Normal style. Finally, you **exported** a style to another document.

Topic D   In this topic, you used styles to create an **outline**. Then you learned how to **organize** and **format** an outline.

Topic E   In this topic, you viewed a document in Full Screen Reading view. You also navigated in the document by using the **Document Map** and **Thumbnails** panes.

Independent practice activity

In this activity, you'll compare the styles of two selections and make them match. Then you'll create a style and apply it. You'll also use that style to create a document outline, and then you'll view the outline. Finally, you'll view the document in Full Screen Reading view.

1 Open Practice styles, from the current unit folder, and save it as **My practice styles**.

2 Use the Reveal Formatting pane to examine the formatting of the heading on page 1. (*Hint*: Press Shift+F1.)

3 Use the Reveal formatting pane to format the heading on page 1 by using the same formatting options that are used for the heading on page 2.

   To do this: First select the heading on page 2. Then, in the Reveal Formatting pane, specify that you want to compare this to another selection. Select the heading on page 1 so that you can see the differences between the headings' formats.

4 Create a style named **Page heading** based on the formatting of the heading on page 1.

5 Set the Page heading style to use outline Level 1.

6 Apply the Page heading style to the headings on pages 2, 3, 4, 6 and 7.

7 View the document in Outline view.

8 View the document in Full Screen Reading view.

9 Display the Document Map and Thumbnails panes.

10 Return to Print Layout view.

11 Close the Styles pane and the Reveal Formatting pane.

12 Update and close the document.

Review questions

1 What keys do you press to open the Reveal Formatting pane?

2 How do you use the Reveal Formatting pane to compare the formatting of two selections?

3 What are some advantages of using styles?

4 What style is applied to a new, blank document by default?

5 You've created a section-heading style named "Appendix Heading." You want this style to have the same formatting as the Heading 1 style, but you want it the new style to make text red. How can you do this without manually specifying every style setting?

6 What happens if you check Automatically update in the Modify Style dialog box?

7 What happens if you delete a style that you've used in a document?

8 How can you use Word's styles to create an outline?

9 If you want to create an outline from a document that uses custom styles, how can you do so?

10 What is the function of the Document Map pane?

11 How can you view a Document Map?

U n i t   2

Sections and columns

Unit time: 60 minutes

Complete this unit, and you'll know how to:

A Create and format sections of text by using section breaks, headers and footers, and page numbering.

B Format text into multiple columns.

Topic A: Creating and formatting sections

This topic covers the following Microsoft Certified Application Specialist exam objectives for Word 2007.

#	Objective
1.2.2	**Create and modify headers and footers (Not using Quick Parts)**
	• Add and modify page numbers in headers and footers (This objective is also covered in *Word 2007: Basic*, in the unit titled "Page layout.")
2.3.2	**Create and modify sections**
	• Insert section breaks
	• Delete section breaks
	• Modify the header and footer for a section

Section breaks

Explanation

Some types of page layout settings, such as margins and page numbering, typically apply to an entire document. Sometimes, though, you might want to use different layouts in different parts of a document. You can do this by dividing the document into sections.

A *section* is a portion of a document in which you can set certain page layout options, such as margins, headers and footers, page numbering, and page orientation. By default, a document has only one section. However, you can create additional sections in a document—and even on a single page—and apply different settings to each one.

Inserting section breaks

To divide a document into sections, you need to insert section breaks. These are inserted as hidden formatting symbols, so they're visible only if the Show/Hide button is selected.

To insert a section break:

1 Place the insertion point where you want to create a new section.
2 On the Page Layout tab, in the Page Setup group, click Breaks to display the Breaks menu, shown in Exhibit 2-1. Then choose the kind of section break you want to insert.

There are four types of section breaks:

- Next Page — Starts a new section on the next page.
- Continuous — Starts a new section on the same page.
- Even Page — Starts a new section on the next even-numbered page.
- Odd Page — Starts a new section on the next odd-numbered page.

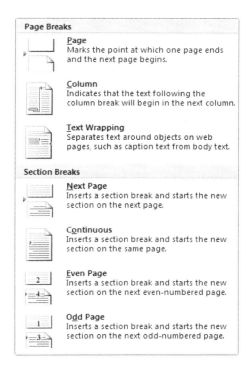

Exhibit 2-1: The Breaks menu

Deleting section breaks

To delete a section break in most views, place the insertion point just before the break and press Delete. In Draft view, click the section break to select it, and then press Delete.

A-1:   Inserting and deleting section breaks

Here's how	Here's why
1 Open Spice info	From the current unit folder.
Save the document as **My spice info**	In the current unit folder.
2 Scroll through the document	It begins with a letter from the chairman, followed by a table of contents, a history of spices, and spice descriptions, and ending with a collection of recipes. Each portion of the document is separated with page breaks. You will insert section breaks.
Switch to Draft view	On the View tab, in the Document Views group, click Draft.
3 At the bottom of page 1, select the page break	Click it.
Press (DELETE)	To delete the page break. The insertion point now is at the beginning of the heading "Contents."
4 Activate the Page Layout tab	
In the Page Setup group, click **Breaks**	To display a menu with options for page and section breaks.
Under Section Breaks, choose **Next Page**	To create a section that starts on the next page.
5 At the bottom of page 2, delete the page break	Click the page break to select it and press Delete.
Insert a Next Page section break	(In the Page Setup group, from the Breaks menu, choose Next Page.) To move the text so that it starts on a new page.
6 At the bottom of page 3, delete the page break	
Insert a Next Page section break	To move "The medicinal use of spices" so that it starts in a new section. However, this information is actually part of "The long history of spices" and shouldn't be separated by a section break.
7 At the bottom of page 3, click the section break	To select it.
Press (DELETE)	To remove the section break.

8 In the Page Setup group, click
Breaks

Under Page Breaks, choose **Page**   To reinsert the page break at the bottom of page 3. There are page breaks at the bottom of pages 3 and 4. You'll leave them there because those pages are part of the same section.

9 On page 6, place the insertion point before "Bay leaf"   The Spice Name style is applied to this heading. The style includes formatting that inserts a page break before the heading automatically, so you can't delete the page break here.

Insert a Next Page section break   (In the Page Setup group, from the Breaks menu, choose Next Page.) The section break replaces the page break.

10 Create a section that starts on page 15   (The page with the recipe "Spicy Buzzard Wings.") Delete the page break on page 14, and insert a section break that starts the new section on the next page.

11 Update the document

Section formatting

Explanation

You can apply different types of page layout settings to different sections. For example, you can change the orientation and apply different margins and borders to each section. To change the page layout for a section, first make sure the insertion point is in that section.

To change the page layout for an entire document when it contains sections:

1 Open the Page Setup dialog box.
2 From the Apply to list, select Whole document.
3 Specify the desired settings and click OK.

Do it!

A-2: Formatting sections

Here's how	Here's why
1 Place the insertion point in the first section	(On page 1). You will set new margins for only that section.
In the Page Setup group, from the Margins list, select **Wide**	To change the left and right margins to 2 inches.
Scroll in the document	Notice that Word has applied the new margin settings to only the first section.
2 Place the insertion point in the first section	If necessary.
Click **Margins** and choose **Custom Margins...**	To open the Page Setup dialog box with the Margins tab activated. You will specify custom margins.
3 Edit the Top box to read **2**	
Edit the Left box to read **1.25**	
Edit the Right box to read **1.25**	
4 In the Apply to list, verify that "This section" is selected	These changes will be applied to only the current section.
Click **OK**	To close the dialog box and apply the margin settings.
5 Update the document	

Section headers and footers

Explanation

When you insert a header or footer in a section, that header or footer is applied by default to the entire document. For example, if you insert a header in the third section of a document with five sections, that header will appear in all five sections. To format the headers and footers differently for different sections, you have to remove the links between sections. To do so, activate the Header & Footer Tools; then, in the Navigation group, click the Link to Previous button. Doing so removes the link between the current header or footer and the ones in previous sections. However, subsequent headers and footers (if any exist) will still be linked to the current one.

While headers and footers are linked, any text you type in one header or footer will appear in all headers or footers. After they are unlinked, you can edit and format them independently. However, any text you've already entered and any formatting you've already applied will remain in the other headers and footers until you change them.

To tell whether a section header or footer is linked, check the top-right corner of the header or footer area, as shown in Exhibit 2-2.

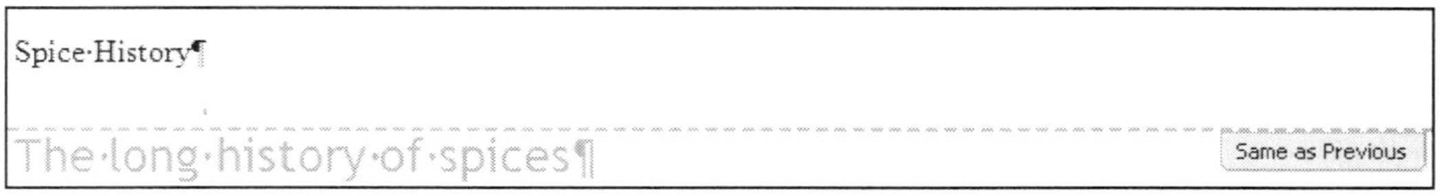

Spice·History¶

The·long·history·of·spices¶

Same as Previous

Exhibit 2-2: A linked header

Do it!   **A-3:   Inserting section headers and footers**

Here's how	Here's why
1 Click in the third section of the document	The part that begins with the heading "The long history of spices."
2 Activate the Insert tab	
In the Header & Footer group, click **Header**	
Choose **Edit Header**	To display the header area. The header is labeled "Header –Section 3-."
3 Type **Spice History**	
4 Observe the right side of the header	

Same as Previous

The text "Same as Previous" indicates that this section's header is linked to the header of the previous section. You'll remove the link so that you can edit each section's header separately.

5 In the Navigation group, click **Link to Previous**	To remove the link between the Section 3 header and the previous section header. The text "Same as Previous" is gone.
6 Click **Previous Section**	To go to the Section 2 header. Because you entered text in the header before you removed the link, that text appears in the Section 1 and 2 headers.
Delete the contents of the Section 2 header	
7 Go to the Section 1 header	(Click Previous Section.) Because the Section 1 and 2 headers are linked, when you deleted the text from the Section 2 header, the text in the Section 1 header was also deleted.
8 Go to the Section 4 header	(Click Next Section three times.) This section's header is linked to the previous section's header, so the text you entered there appears here as well.
Remove the link to the previous section's header	In the Navigation group, click the Link to Previous button.
Edit the header text to read **Spice Descriptions**	

9 Remove the link between the Section 5 and Section 4 headers

Move to the Section 5 header and click the Link to Previous button.

Edit the text in the Section 5 header to read **Recipes**

10 Update the document

Section page numbers

Explanation

Whenever you use the Insert Page Number command to insert page numbers, Word automatically inserts page numbers starting at 1 and continuing consecutively through a document. For some documents, however, you might need more complex numbering. For example, many books contain introductory material that is numbered with Roman numerals—"page 1" doesn't actually begin until several physical pages into the book.

You can tell Word how to format page numbers for different sections by using the Page Number Format dialog box, shown in Exhibit 2-3. Word will number linked sections consecutively, but format them independently. For example, if you insert a page number in the first section—and that section is linked to the second section—then the page number will appear in the first and second sections. However, if you use the Page Number Format dialog box to change the number format for the first section, the formatting will apply to only the first section, and not the second. Likewise, if you insert page numbers in subsequent, unlinked sections, Word will continue numbering pages consecutively unless you specify otherwise in the Page Number Format dialog box.

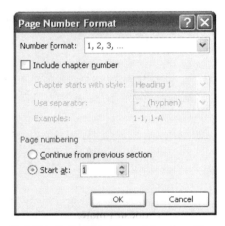

Exhibit 2-3: The Page Number Format dialog box

Do it!   **A-4: Formatting section page numbers**

Here's how	Here's why
1 Move to the Section 1 header	You'll format this page and the contents page to use lowercase Roman numerals as page numbers.
2 In the Header & Footer group, click **Page Number**	
Choose **Top of Page**	To display page number options.
Select **Plain Number 3**	(You might need to scroll.) To insert a page number on the right side of the header.
3 In the Header & Footer group, click **Page Number**	On the Design tab.
Choose **Format Page Numbers...**	To open the Page Number Format dialog box.
From the Number format list, select **i, ii, iii ...**	To use lowercase Roman numerals, which are commonly used to number introductory pages in books.
Click **OK**	To close the dialog box.
4 Move to the Section 2 header	
Observe the page number	Even though the page is numbered 2, the format doesn't match the first page because this is a separate section.
For the second section, set the page number format to **i, ii, iii, ...**	In the Header & Footer group, click Format Page Numbers to open the Page Number Format dialog box. Select the format from the Number format list and click OK.
5 Move to the Section 3 header	It begins on page 3. You'll insert a page number and set it to use Arabic numerals.
In the header, place the insertion point after "Spice History" as shown	Spice·History¶
Insert a page number with the style **Plain Number 3**	In the Header & Footer group, click Page Number, choose Top of Page, and select the style.
	Notice that the current header text has been removed. You'll fix this next.
On the left side of the header, type **Spice History**	Click the left side of the header and type.

6 Select the page number in the header	This page is numbered 3. You'll change the numbering to start with 1 on this page.
Open the Page Number Format dialog box	In the Header & Footer group, click Page Number and choose Format Page Numbers.
Under Page numbering, select **Start at**	To have the page numbering start at page 1 in this section.
Click **OK**	
7 In Sections 4 and 5, insert a page number with the format **1, 2, 3, …**	(Select and copy the existing header text first. After adding the page number, you can paste the text on the left side of the header to reinsert it.)
	Section 4 begins on page 6, and Section 5 begins on page 15. When you insert the page numbers, the first page in Section 4 will be numbered as page 4, and the first page in Section 5 will be numbered as page 13.
8 Double-click in the document area	To close the header and footer areas.
9 Update the document	

Topic B: Working with columns

This topic covers the following Microsoft Certified Application Specialist exam objective for Word 2007.

#	Objective
1.2.3	**Create and format columns**
	• Select the number of columns
	• Column width and spacing

Formatting text into columns

Explanation

Newsletters, brochures, and reports often present content in columns. Using columns can save space and enable you to present more information on a page, as shown in Exhibit 2-4. This can help reduce the page count of a long document.

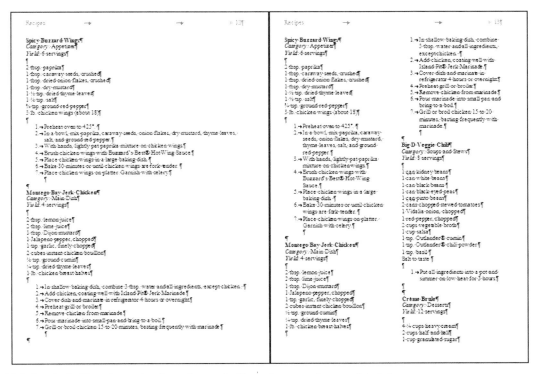

Exhibit 2-4: Text in a single column (left) and two columns (right)

You can view multiple columns in Print Layout view and Full Screen Reading view.

To format text into columns:

1 Select the text you want to format as columns. (Drag to select the text. Or, if you want to format an entire section, place the insertion point in that section.)

2 On the Page Layout tab, in the Page Setup group, click Columns and choose More Columns to open the Columns dialog box, shown in Exhibit 2-5.

3 Under Presets, select a format. If you need more than three columns, enter the value in the Number of columns box.

4 Adjust the width and spacing of the columns as required. (As you change the various settings in this dialog box, observe the Preview area to get an idea of how the selected text will look.)

5 Click OK.

You can also create columns by using the options in the Columns gallery in the Page Setup group.

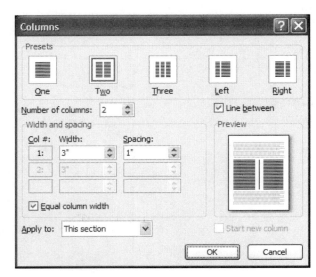

Exhibit 2-5: The Columns dialog box

Adjusting the spacing between columns

You can adjust the spacing between columns to provide balance. For example, if the columns are too close together, the text might be difficult to read. If there's too much white space, the column text might appear to be falling off the page. To adjust the spacing:

1 Select the columns between which you want to adjust the spacing.

2 Open the Columns dialog box.

3 Under Width and spacing, in the Spacing box, enter the desired measurement (in inches). The Width box adjusts to accommodate the new spacing.

4 Click OK.

Do it! **B-1: Formatting text into columns**

Here's how	Here's why
1 Place the insertion point in any of the recipes	In the last section of the document, beginning on page 15.
2 Activate the Page Layout tab	
In the Page Setup group, click **Columns**	To display the Columns gallery.
Select **Two**	To have the text flow into two columns.
3 Scroll through the document	The column settings were applied to the last section only.
4 Place the insertion point in the last section of the document	If necessary.
From the Margins gallery, select **Normal**	To narrow the left and right margins.
Click **Columns** and choose **More Columns...**	To open the Columns dialog box.
5 Check **Line between**	To add a vertical line between the columns.
Edit the Spacing box for column 1 to read **1**	
	To set the space between the columns to 1 inch.
Press ⬚TAB⬚	Notice that the column width changed when you set a new Spacing value.
6 Click **OK**	To apply the column settings.
7 Update the document	

Width and spacing

Col #:	Width:	Spacing:
1:	3"	1"

Inserting and deleting column breaks

Explanation

A *column break* is a mark that indicates the end of a column. When one of the columns is longer than the other, you can insert a column break to balance the columns. The text after the break will move to the next column. You might also want to start a paragraph at the beginning of a column or move a heading to the next column to improve readability.

To insert a column break:

   1   Place the insertion point where you want to insert the column break.

   2   Activate the Page Layout tab.

   3   In the Page Setup group, click Breaks and choose Column.

To delete a column break, place the insertion point just before the break and press Delete. When the column break is deleted, the text shifts to the previous column.

Do it!

B-2: Inserting column breaks

Here's how	Here's why
1 Place the insertion point to the left of "Montego Bay Jerk Chicken"	The second recipe, in the left column on page 15.
2 Activate the Page Layout tab	If necessary.
In the Page Setup group, from the Breaks menu, choose **Column**	To insert a column break. The text moves to the right column.
3 Insert a column break before "Big D Veggie Chile"	From the Breaks menu, choose Column.
4 Insert column breaks before the Crème Brûlée and Wasabi Pork Tenderloin recipes	
5 Update the document	

Creating a heading that spans columns

Explanation

Even though you have text laid out in columns, you might want a heading that stretches across all of them, instead of across just one column. To add a heading that spans columns and uses the width of the page:

1 Place the insertion point where you want the heading to appear, and type the heading text.

2 Insert a Continuous section break after the text.

3 Place the insertion point in the section with the heading.

4 Set the number of columns to one.

Do it!

B-3:   Adding a heading across columns

Here's how	Here's why
1 Place the insertion point before "Spicy Buzzard Wings"	On page 15.
Type **Cooking with Outlander Spices**	
2 With the insertion point after the text you just typed, display the Breaks menu and choose **Continuous**	To create a section break that doesn't break across pages or columns.
3 Press ⬅	To move the insertion point to the end of the heading line.
Set the number of columns to 1	(In the Columns gallery, select One.) To make the heading span both columns.
Press ↵ ENTER twice	To insert a blank line after the heading.
4 Place the insertion point in the line **Cooking with Outlander Spices**	
Center the text horizontally	(On the Home tab, in the Paragraph group, click the Center button.) The heading uses one column instead of two.
5 Update and close the document	

Unit summary: Sections and columns

Topic A   In this topic, you learned how to insert and delete **section breaks**. Then you formatted pages in a section. Next, you inserted section headers and footers. You also formatted section page numbers.

Topic B   In this topic, you formatted text into **columns**. You learned how to insert **column breaks**, and you added a heading that spans multiple columns.

Independent practice activity

In this activity, you'll create sections in a document. Then you'll insert page numbers and format them in different sections. You'll also format some text into columns.

1 Open Practice sections, from the current unit folder, and save it as **My practice sections**.

2 Create new sections beginning on pages 2, 3, 4, 7, and 8. (Skip pages 5 and 6 for now.) (*Hint*: Delete the page breaks before creating the sections.)

3 On page 4, select the page break and insert a section break that begins the new section on the next page. (*Hint*: Don't delete the original page break. Page 5 contains a graphic—deleting the page break and then inserting a section break will cause the graphic to be placed incorrectly on the page.)

4 Delete the page break that appears at the top of page 5.

5 In the header section of each page, on the right side, insert the page number.

6 Format the page number for page 1 as a lowercase Roman numeral. (*Hint*: First, remove the link between this section and the next.)

7 Format the page numbering to begin at "1" on the second page of the document.

8 In the section that begins on page 8, format the text so that it appears in two columns.

9 Insert a column break so that page 8 appears as shown in Exhibit 2-6.

10 Format the heading on page 8 so that it spans both columns. (*Hint*: After inserting the section break, an extra paragraph mark will appear in the first column; delete it.)

11 Update and close the document.

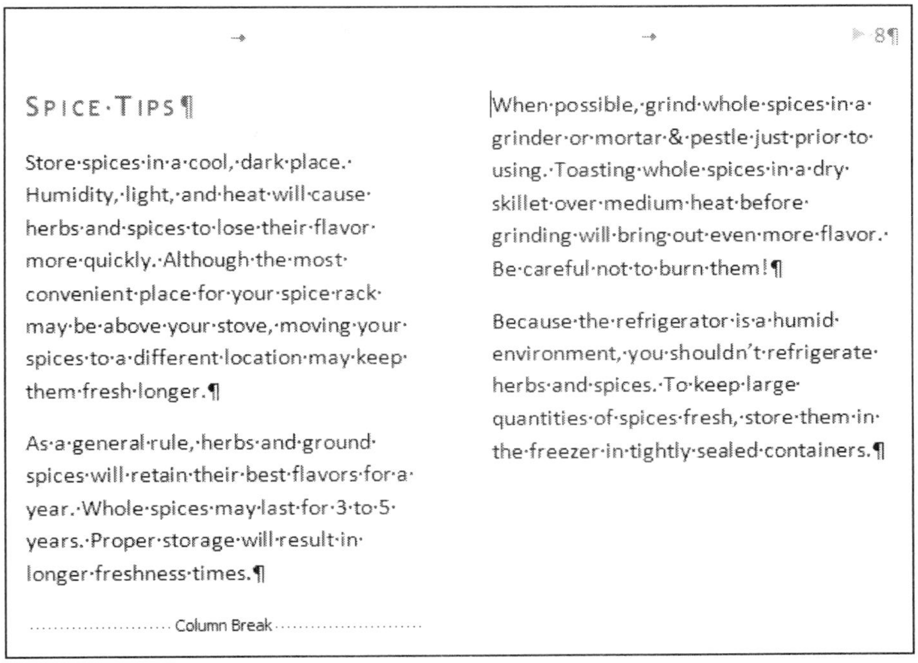

SPICE·TIPS¶

Store·spices·in·a·cool,·dark·place.· Humidity,·light,·and·heat·will·cause· herbs·and·spices·to·lose·their·flavor· more·quickly.·Although·the·most· convenient·place·for·your·spice·rack· may·be·above·your·stove,·moving·your· spices·to·a·different·location·may·keep· them·fresh·longer.¶

As·a·general·rule,·herbs·and·ground· spices·will·retain·their·best·flavors·for·a· year.·Whole·spices·may·last·for·3·to·5· years.·Proper·storage·will·result·in· longer·freshness·times.¶

.... Column Break ....

When·possible,·grind·whole·spices·in·a· grinder·or·mortar·&·pestle·just·prior·to· using.·Toasting·whole·spices·in·a·dry· skillet·over·medium·heat·before· grinding·will·bring·out·even·more·flavor.· Be·careful·not·to·burn·them!¶

Because·the·refrigerator·is·a·humid· environment,·you·shouldn't·refrigerate· herbs·and·spices.·To·keep·large· quantities·of·spices·fresh,·store·them·in· the·freezer·in·tightly·sealed·containers.¶

Exhibit 2-6: Page 8 as it appears after Step 9 of the independent practice activity

Review questions

1 Why might you want to create sections?

2 What are the four types of section breaks?

3 Your document is divided into five sections, and you want to create a header in the third section. By default, any text that you enter is applied to the headers in which of the following?

A Any sections that come after the current section

B Any sections that come before the current section

C Only the current section

D Every section in the document

4 How do you change the spacing between columns?

5 How do you position a heading so that it spans columns?

Unit 3

Formatting tables

Unit time: 60 minutes

Complete this unit, and you'll know how to:

A Align text in a table, merge and split table cells, change text orientation in a table, and resize rows.

B Change table borders and apply shading to cells.

C Sort data in a table, split a table, repeat a header row on multiple pages, and enter a formula in a table.

D Apply and modify table styles.

Topic A: Table formatting basics

This topic covers the following Microsoft Certified Application Specialist exam objectives for Word 2007.

#	Objective
4.3.3	Merge and split table cells
4.3.5	Change the position and direction of cell contents

Aligning table text

Explanation

Because tabular information is sometimes difficult to read, some formatting might help to direct your audience's attention to particular areas of a table, making it easier for them to follow and process the information. For example, you can align text in cells, merge cells, apply borders and shading to cells, and change text orientation.

When you enter text in a table cell, Word aligns the text to the upper-left corner by default. You can change text alignment by using buttons in the Alignment group, shown in Exhibit 3-1, on the Table Tools | Layout tab. You can change the text alignment for every cell in a table or for only selected cells. To change the alignment for a selected cell, place the insertion point in the cell and click one of the alignment buttons in the Alignment group. To change the text alignment for every cell in a table, select the table and select an alignment option.

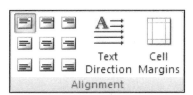

Exhibit 3-1: The Alignment group

Do it!

A-1:   Aligning text in table cells

Here's how	Here's why
1 Open Kiosk locations	From the current unit folder.
Save the document as **My kiosk locations**	In the current unit folder.
2 Select the top row of the table	Point to the left of the row and double-click to select the header row. The Table Tools appear, adding the Design and Layout tabs to the Ribbon.
3 Activate the Layout tab	
In the Alignment group, click ≡	(The Align Center Left button.) To center the text in the header row vertically, and have it left-aligned horizontally.
4 Drag to select the cells containing the numbers in the table's right column, as shown	Projected·Revenues·($·in·thousands)¤ 47¤ 62¤ 56¤ 71¤ 102¤ 83¤ 40¤ 38¤ 165¤ 95¤ 88¤ 132¤ 52¤ 53¤ 27¤
On the Layout tab, click ≡	(The Align Center icon.) To center the text.
5 Update the document	

Merging cells

Explanation

You can merge cells when you want their contents to span more than one cell. *Merging cells* means combining two or more cells in the same row or column to form a single cell. For example, you might have empty cells that you want to merge into one cell; doing so makes a table less "busy" and helps direct your audience's attention to important information.

To merge cells in a table, select the cells you want to merge. Then, in the Merge group, on the Table Tools | Layout tab, click Merge Cells. You can also right-click and choose Merge Cells from the shortcut menu.

Do it!   **A-2:   Merging table cells**

Here's how	Here's why
1 Delete "MD" from the first cell of the third row	(Below the first MD row.) Three cells contain the same information. You'll delete the redundant text and merge the cells into one.
Delete "MD" from the first cell of the fourth row	
2 Select the three cells as shown	MD¤ / ¤ / ¤
3 In the Merge group, click **Merge Cells**	Merge Cells / Split Cells / Split Table / Merge
	(On the Layout tab.) To merge the three cells into one. It's now easier to see which cities are in Maryland.
4 Delete "NJ" from the second and third NJ cells	
Merge the three cells, as shown	NJ¤ — Atlantic·City¤ / Cherry·Hill¤ / Trenton¤
	Select the three cells, and in the Merge group, click Merge Cells.
5 Remove the remaining duplicate state abbreviations, and merge the cells for each state, as shown	MD¤ — Baltimore¤ / Bethesda¤ / Rockville¤ ; NJ¤ — Atlantic·City¤ / Cherry·Hill¤ / Trenton¤ ; NY¤ — Albany¤ / Buffalo¤ / New·York¤ / New·York¤ ; PA¤ — Harrisburg¤ / Philadelphia¤ ; VA¤ — Charlottesville¤ / Fairfax¤ / Richmond¤
6 Update the document	

Splitting cells

Explanation

You might also need to *split* a cell, dividing it into two or more cells, creating new rows and/or columns. For example, if you need to add a cell to a section of a table, but you don't want to add an entire row or column, you can split the cell.

To split a cell:

1   Place the insertion point in the cell you want to split.

2   In the Merge group, on the Table Tools | Layout tab, click Split Cells to open the Split Cells dialog box.

3   Enter the number of columns and rows you want to create from the selected cell.

4   Click OK.

Do it!   **A-3: Splitting table cells**

Here's how	Here's why
1 Open City sales	From the current unit folder.
Save the document as **My city sales**	(In the current unit folder.) You want to insert a column that will list the sales manager for each state.
2 Verify that the insertion point is in the first column	The leftmost column in the table.
3 Activate the Layout tab	Under Table Tools.
In the Rows & Columns group, click **Insert Right**	Word inserts a column with 24 rows, corresponding with the layout of the table before the cells in the left column were merged.
	Rather than merging each group of cells to correspond with the states, you want to create a column that has the same layout as the State column.
Press CTRL + Z	To undo the last action.
4 Select the State column	(Be sure to select the entire column.) You'll split each cell in the column into two, in effect creating a new column that corresponds with the State column.
5 In the Merge group, click **Split Cells**	To open the Split Cells dialog box.
Verify that the Number of columns box reads 2	After the split, you'll have two columns.
Clear **Merge cells before split**	If you don't clear this option, Word will merge the cells in the State column and divide the contents into two cells.
	The Number of rows box becomes dimmed.
Click **OK**	To split the cells into two columns.
6 In the top cell of the new column, enter **Sales Manager**	
7 Update and close the document	

Changing the orientation of text

Explanation

To improve the readability of data in a table, you might need to change its orientation. By default, Word aligns text horizontally. To change the orientation of text in a table:

1 Select the cell(s) whose orientation you want to change.
2 On the Layout tab, in the Alignment group, click Text Direction.

- If the text is originally displayed horizontally (read from left to right), then clicking once will change the orientation to vertical (read from top to bottom).
- Clicking twice will switch the direction of the vertical orientation so that the text is read from bottom to top.
- Clicking a third time will restore the text to its original position.

Do it!

A-4:   Changing text orientation

Here's how	Here's why
1 Switch to the My kiosk locations document	If necessary.
2 Place the insertion point in any cell in the first column	
Activate the Layout tab	If necessary.
In the Rows & Columns group, click **Insert Left**	To add a new column to the left of the table. Word automatically selects the new column.
3 Merge all of the cells in the column	In the Merge group, click Merge Cells.
4 In the left column, enter **Mid-Atlantic Region Kiosks**	
5 In the Alignment group, click **Text Direction** twice	The text now flows vertically from the bottom to the top of the table.
6 In the Alignment group, click ▯	(The Align Center Left icon.) Note that the icons in the Alignment group have changed to reflect the new text direction.
In the Cell Size group, from the AutoFit list, select **AutoFit Contents**	To narrow the width of the column.
7 Update the document	

Resizing rows

Explanation

By default, Word automatically adjusts the size of a cell to fit its contents, but you might want to increase or decrease a cell's default size. You can change the size of table rows by dragging the cell boundaries or by adjusting the settings in the Cell Size group.

To change the row height, point to the row boundary; when the pointer becomes a double-headed arrow, drag up or down. To specify a row's height precisely, first place the insertion point in the row whose height you want to change. Then, in the Cell Size group, enter a value in the Height box.

Do it!

A-5: Changing row height

Here's how	Here's why
1 Select the cells in the header row	Do not include the left column of merged cells.
2 In the Cell Size group, edit the Height box to read **0.5**	 To increase the row height.
3 Select the cells with the city, store location, and revenue information, as shown	
In the Cell Size group, click the up-arrow until the value in the Height box is **0.3**	All of the selected rows change, as well as the merged cells containing the states.
4 Update the document	

Topic B: Borders and shading

This topic covers the following Microsoft Certified Application Specialist exam objective for Word 2007.

#	Objective
4.3.2	**Modify table properties and options**
	• Apply borders and shading

Table borders

Explanation

After you've created a table, you can apply borders and shading to highlight cells, rows, columns, or the entire table. By using the formatting options available in the Table Styles and Draw Borders groups, you can apply borders of different widths and styles, and you can apply borders to different areas of a table. You can also apply shading of different colors to selected cells.

To apply borders:

1 Select the cells you want to apply the border to, or select the entire table.

2 On the Table Tools | Design tab, select options in the Draw Borders group:
   • From the Line Style list, select a border style.
   • From the Line Weight list, select a thickness.
   • From the Pen Color list, select a color.

3 In the Table Styles group, select an option from the Borders menu, shown in Exhibit 3-2, to apply the border with the selected formatting to specific areas of the table.

Exhibit 3-2: The Borders menu

Do it!   **B-1:   Changing table borders**

Here's how	Here's why

1 Select the indicated cells

	State	City	Store Location	Projected Revenues (\$ in thousands)
Mid-Atlantic Region Kiosks	MD	Baltimore	Prestige Market	47
		Bethesda	Prestige Market	62
		Rockville	Mediterranean Gourmet	56
	NJ	Atlantic City	Roma	71
		Cherry Hill	Patterson's Grocers	102
		Trenton	Roma	83
	NY	Albany	Prestige Market	40
		Buffalo	Mediterranean Gourmet	38
		New York	Patterson's Grocers	165
		New York	Village Gourmet Bakery and Grocer	95
	PA	Harrisburg	Patterson's Grocers	88
		Philadelphia	Patterson's Grocers	132
	VA	Charlottesville	Roma	52
		Fairfax	Mediterranean Gourmet	53
		Richmond	Prestige Market	27

2 Activate the Design tab

Under Table Tools.

In the Draw Borders group, from the Line Weight list, select **2 1/4 pt**

3 In the Table Styles group, from the Borders menu, choose **Outside Borders**

To apply the new line weight to the outside border of the selected group of cells.

4 Click in the left column of the table

(The column with the vertical text.) You will remove the border from the top, bottom, and left sides of the column.

5 In the Draw Borders group. from the
Line Style list, select **No Border**

In the Table Styles group, from the Borders menu, choose **Top Border**	To remove the top border.
From the Borders menu, choose **Left Border**	To remove the left border.
From the Borders menu, choose **Bottom Border**	To remove the bottom border.

6 Update the document

Cell shading

Explanation

You might want to highlight some sections of a table to visually differentiate them from other sections, as shown in Exhibit 3-3. You can apply shading to do so. You can apply shading to the entire table or to specific cells. To do so, first select the cells you want to shade. Then, on the Design tab, in the Table Styles group, select a color from the Shading gallery.

State¤	City¤	Store·Location¤	Projected·Revenues·($·in·thousands)¤
MD¤	Baltimore¤	Prestige·Market¤	47¤
	Bethesda¤	Prestige·Market¤	62¤

Exhibit 3-3: Shaded cells in a table

Do it!

B-2: Shading table cells

Here's how	Here's why
1 Select the cells in the header row, as shown	State¤ City¤ Store·Location¤ Projected·Revenues·($·in·thousands)¤
2 In the Table Styles group, from the Shading gallery, select the indicated green color	**Theme Colors** Olive Green, Accent 3, Lighter 40%.
3 Deselect the row	To observe the shading color.
4 View the document in Print Preview	(Click the Office button and choose Print, Print Preview.) To view your table as it will appear in print.
Close the Preview window	(On the Print Preview tab, in the Preview group, click Close Print Preview.) To return to Print Layout view.
5 Update and close the document	

Topic C: Table data

This topic covers the following Microsoft Certified Application Specialist exam objectives for Word 2007.

#	Objective
4.2.2	**Sort content**
	• Sort table contents
4.3.4	**Perform calculations in tables**

Sorting data in a table

Explanation

Tables in Word have some of the same functionality as tables in Excel. For example, you can sort data, and you can insert equations in table cells. For more complex operations, however, you should use a spreadsheet program like Excel.

You can use the Sort command to organize table information in a particular order. To do so, first select the rows to be organized. Then, in the Data group (on the Layout tab), click Sort to open the Sort dialog box, shown in Exhibit 3-4. By default, the selected data is sorted alphabetically in ascending order. You can also sort numerically or chronologically.

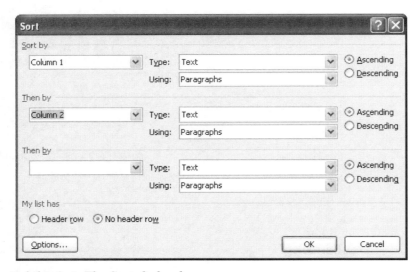

Exhibit 3-4: The Sort dialog box

Do it!   ## C-1:   Sorting table data

Here's how	Here's why
1 Open Sorting	From the current unit folder
Save the document as **My sorting**	In the current unit folder.
Observe the table data	The states and cities aren't listed in alphabetical order.
2 Select all of the table rows except the header row	
3 Activate the Layout tab	
In the Data group, click **Sort**	To open the Sort dialog box. You'll sort first by state and then by city.
4 From the Sort by list, select **Column 1**	(If necessary.) To have the table rows sorted initially by state.
From the Then by list, select **Column 2**	To have the table rows within each state sorted by city.
Click **OK**	To sort the table data.
5 Open the Sort dialog box	Click the Sort button.
In the Sort by list, select **Column 3**	Number appears in the Type box because the information in column 3 is numeric.
From the Then by list, select **(none)**	You no longer want to perform a secondary sort on Column 2 data.
Click **OK**	To sort the data in ascending order by the values in column 3.
6 Open the Sort dialog box	
Under Sort by, select **Descending**	
Click **OK**	To sort the values in descending order.
7 Update and close the document	

Splitting tables

Explanation

You might be working with one table that you want to split into two. For example, you might want to sort different sections of a table or show sections separately, with text in between. To split a table:

1 Place the insertion point where you want to split the table. The selected row will be the first row of the new table.

2 In the Merge group (on the Layout tab), click Split Table.

Do it!

C-2: Splitting a table

Here's how	Here's why
1 Open Split table	From the current unit folder.
Save the document as **My split table**	(In the current unit folder.) The table contains data from Eastern and Western states. You'll split the table so that you can sort data for each region separately.
2 Click the cell containing "WA"	You'll split the table into eastern and western regional tables.
Activate the Layout tab	
In the Merge group, click **Split Table**	To split the table, with the selected row becoming the top row of the new table.
3 Insert a row at the top of the new table	Place the insertion point in the WA row. On the Layout tab, in the Rows & Columns group, click Insert Above.
4 Copy the header from the first table	Select the three cells containing the column headings and press Ctrl+C.
In the second table, drag to select the cells where you want to paste the header text	Be sure to drag to select the cells. If you use the selection bar to select the row, you'll insert a new row when you paste the information.
Press (CTRL) + (V)	To paste the header text into the top row of the second table.
5 Update and close the document	

Repeat a header row on multiple pages

Explanation

When you have a table that spans multiple pages, you probably want the header row to appear at the top of each page. In Word, the *header row* is the first row in a table, and typically it contains descriptive headings for the data in each column. If the header row appears at the top of each page, people reading the table don't have to flip back to the first page to determine which column they're viewing. However, if you add or remove rows or format the table differently, you'll still want the header to appear at the top of each page, rather than re-flow with the rest of the table.

To do this, make sure that the header you want to use is the top row of the table. Then, with that row selected, open the Table Properties dialog box. Activate the Row tab and check "Repeat as header row at the top of each page."

Do it!

C-3: Repeating the header row

Here's how	Here's why
1 Open Repeat header	From the current unit folder.
Save the document as **My repeat header**	In the current unit folder.
2 Scroll to examine the table	The data continues onto a second page. You want the header to appear at the top of the second page.
Return to the top of the document	Press Ctrl + Home, if necessary.
3 Place the insertion point in the empty row below "Sales report"	You'll split the table so that the next row is the header row. Word automatically identifies the top row of a table as the header.
Split the table	On the Layout tab, in the Merge group, click Split Table.
4 Click in the empty row at the top of the second table	To select it.
In the Rows & Columns group, click **Delete** and choose **Delete Rows**	(On the Layout tab.) To delete the empty row at the top of the table.

Outlander·Spices¤			
Sales·report·¤			
¶			
Product¤	Region¤	Prior·year¤	Current·year¤
Annatto·Seed¤	East¤	$11,771¤	$24,181¤

5 Place the insertion point in the top row of the second table	If necessary.
6 Activate the Layout tab	If necessary.

7	In the Table group, click **Properties**	To open the Table Properties dialog box.
	Activate the Row tab	Click the tab.
	Check **Repeat as header row at the top of each page**	
	Click **OK**	To close the dialog box.
8	Move to page 2	The header appears at the top of the page. If you were to add or remove rows from the first page of the table, the header would still appear at the top of this page, as long as the table continued onto it.
9	Update and close the document	

Using the Formula dialog box

You can perform various calculations in rows and columns by using formulas. A *formula* is used to perform arithmetic operations, such as calculating an average or a sum. You can also copy formulas from one cell to another in a table.

You can create formulas by using the Formula dialog box, shown in Exhibit 3-5. To open the Formula dialog box, activate the Design tab; then, in the Data group, click Formula. In the Formula dialog box:

- A formula is always preceded by an equal sign (=).

- From the Number format list, you can select the format in which you want the result displayed, such as currency or a percentage.

- From the Paste function list, you can select the function that you want to use in the formula. A *function* is a built-in formula used to perform mathematical calculations. For example, the SUM function adds the numbers in the selected cells.

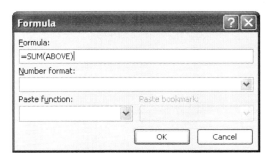

Exhibit 3-5: The Formula dialog box

In Word documents, formulas are treated as fields. When information is subject to change, a *field* is used as a placeholder for that information. For example, a formula that totals a column of numbers is based on the values in the column. If any number in the column changes, the formula needs to reflect the change. In such situations, fields provide the best way to store and display dynamic information.

Calculating totals in rows and columns

Use the SUM function to calculate totals in rows and columns. If the insertion point is in a table containing a series of numbers, the SUM function appears in the Formula dialog box by default. If the insertion point is placed below a cell containing a number, the Formula box will contain =SUM(ABOVE), which adds the numbers in the column. By default, the formula result will have the same formatting as the numbers used in the calculation.

C-4:   Entering a formula in a table

Here's how	Here's why
1 Open Quarterly sales	From the current unit folder.
Save the document as **My quarterly sales**	In the current unit folder.
2 In the first table, click the bottom cell of the North America column	The cell is empty.
Activate the Layout tab	Under Table Tools.
In the Data group, click **Formula**	To open the Formula dialog box. You'll use the default formula in the dialog box.
Click **OK**	To insert a sum of the values in the above cells.
3 Insert a total in the bottom row for the Europe sales	Click the blank cell below the Europe cells, click Formula to open the Formula dialog box, and click OK.
4 Insert a total for Pacific Rim sales	
5 Update the document	

Topic D: Table styles

This topic covers the following Microsoft Certified Application Specialist exam objective for Word 2007.

#	Objective
4.3.1	Apply Quick Styles to tables

Applying styles to tables

Explanation

You already know that you can apply styles to paragraphs by using the Styles gallery. Similarly, you can apply styles to tables by using the Table Styles gallery, accessible from the Table Tools | Design tab. Word provides several style formats you can use to display information in different kinds of tables.

You might want to highlight specific columns or rows, or you might want to shade alternate columns or rows to make reading the data easier. You can do this manually, but you might also be able to use one of Word's table styles, shown in Exhibit 3-6.

To apply a style to a table, first place the insertion point in the table. Then, in the Table Styles group, select a style from the Table Styles gallery.

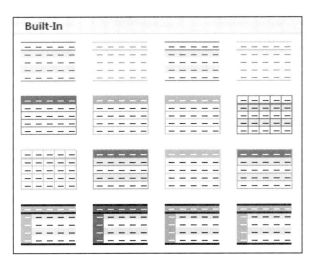

Exhibit 3-6: The Table Styles gallery

Do it!

D-1: Applying table styles

Here's how	Here's why
1 Click any cell in the first table	
2 Activate the Design tab	
3 In the Table Styles group, point to any table style	(Do not click the mouse button). As you point to each style, the document displays the resulting table format in the document window.
Click the style of your choice	To apply that style to the table.
4 Update the document	

Customizing table styles

Explanation

If the styles in the Table Styles gallery don't quite work for the data in your table, you can quickly select options that might correct the problem. For example, you might want to select a style because you like the shading and font; however, maybe you don't want the first column to be formatted differently, which that style does by default. To solve that problem, you can clear the First Column checkbox in the Table Style Options group. The Table Style Options group also contains several other alternatives for customizing a table style.

Do it!

D-2: Using style options

Here's how	Here's why
1 Click the first table	If necessary.
2 In the Table Styles group, click as shown	(The More button.) To expand the gallery.
From the gallery, select the Medium Shading 2 – Accent 4 style	(Use the ScreenTips to find this style.) Notice that this style formats the last column differently than the other two columns of data. You want to use this style, but you don't want the last column formatted differently.
3 In the Table Style Options group, clear **Last Column**	To format the first column so it's the same as the others.
4 Update the document	

Using the Modify Style dialog box

Explanation

To customize a table style even further, you can use the Modify Style dialog box. To do so, expand the Table Styles gallery and choose Modify Table Style to open the Modify Style dialog box, shown in Exhibit 3-7. The Modify Style dialog box for tables is similar to the one for text.

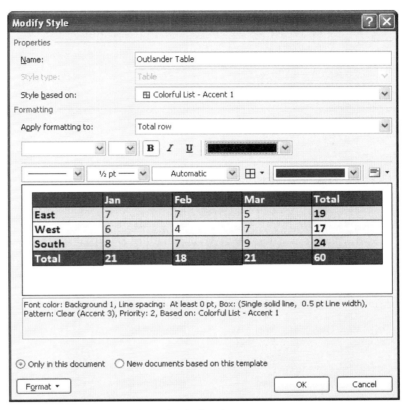

Exhibit 3-7: The Modify Style dialog box

D-3: Modifying a table style

Here's how	Here's why
1 Click in the second table	
2 Expand the Table Style gallery	In the Table Styles group, click the More arrow.
3 Choose **Modify Table Style...**	To open the Modify Style dialog box.
Edit the Name box to read **Outlander Table**	To name the modified style.
From the Style based on list, select **Colorful List – Accent 1**	You'll change the fill color and text color of the header row.
4 Under Formatting, from the Apply formatting to list, select **Header row**	
From the Fill Color list, select the dark green color, as shown	(Olive Green, Accent 3, Darker 50%.) You'll apply a light green shade to the odd rows of the table.
5 From the Apply formatting to list, select **Odd banded rows**	
From the Fill Color list, select the light green color, as shown	Olive Green, Accent 3, Lighter 60%.
6 Apply the dark green color to the fill for the Total row	From the Apply formatting to list, select Total row, and select the dark green color (Olive Green, Accent 3, Darker 50%) from the Fill Color list.
Apply a font color of white to the Total row	
Click **OK**	To apply the new style to the selected table.

7 Click any cell in the first table

   In the Table Styles group, click   (It's now the first style in the gallery.) To apply
   the Outlander Table style   it to the first table.

8 Update and close the document

Unit summary: Formatting tables

Topic A   In this topic, you learned how to **align text** in a table, and you changed the **orientation** of text in a table cell. You also **merged** and **split** table cells, and you **resized rows** in a table.

Topic B   In this topic, you changed a table's **borders** and applied **shading** to table cells.

Topic C   In this topic, you used the Sort dialog box to **sort data** in a table. You also learned how to **split** a table and how to **repeat a header row** on multiple pages. Finally, you learned how to enter **formulas** in a table.

Topic D   In this topic, you applied and modified **table styles**.

Independent practice activity

In this activity, you'll format a table by aligning data in a column, applying a border, and applying a shade to selected cells. Then you'll sort the table data and insert a formula. Finally, you'll apply a table style.

1 Open Table formatting practice (from the current unit folder), and save it as **My table formatting practice**.

2 Align the data in the Earnings column as **Align Center Right**.

3 To the header row (the row containing the column headings), apply a border that is a solid line, 1.5 pt thick.

4 Shade the header row with a light blue color.

5 Sort the table by earnings, starting with the highest salary. (*Hint*: Remember to select all of the rows and columns, except the header row, before opening the Sort dialog box.)

6 Split the table so that the header row appears at the top of the second table.

7 Format the table so that the header row always appears at the top of the second page. (*Hint*: Delete the extra row after splitting the table.)

8 Insert a new row at the bottom of the table.

9 In the rightmost cell of the last row, insert a formula that calculates the total of the salaries shown in the column. Adjust the column width, if necessary.

10 Apply a style of your choice from the Table Styles gallery to the table.

11 Format the style to include a header row. (*Hint*: Check Header Row in the Quick Style Options group.)

12 Update and close the document.

Review questions

1   What is the definition of merging cells?

2   You have a table that contains merged cells, and you want to add a new row in only one cell. How can you do this?

3   What three attributes for formatting a border are found in the Draw Borders group?

4   In the Sort dialog box, you have three options for how to sort data. One is alphabetically. What are the other two?

5   You have a table containing data that you want separated into two separate tables at a specific point. How can you do this?

6   Where can you find the setting for repeating the header row of a table?

7   You've applied a table style to a table, but the style formats the header row differently than the rest of the table. You want it formatted the same as the other rows. Where would you look to find settings to adjust a table style quickly?

8   You want to customize a table style beyond what is available on the Ribbon. Where are these settings located?

Unit 4
Printing labels and envelopes

Unit time: 30 minutes

Complete this unit, and you'll know how to:

A Prepare and print labels.

B Prepare and print envelopes.

Topic A: Labels

Explanation

After preparing a letter or package to send to an individual or organization, you'll need to create an address label. You can use Word's Envelopes and Labels dialog box to quickly prepare and print an address for an envelope or label of the size you specify.

Printing labels for a single recipient

To print a label by using the Envelopes and Labels dialog box:

1 Open or create a document.

2 Activate the Mailings tab.

3 In the Create group, click Labels to open the Envelopes and Labels dialog box with the Labels tab activated, as shown in Exhibit 4-1.

4 Click Options to open the Label Options dialog box. Specify the printer and label information, and click OK.

5 Under Address (in the Envelopes and Labels dialog box), enter the address you want to print.

6 Click Print to print the document, or click New Document to generate a new document based on the settings you've specified.

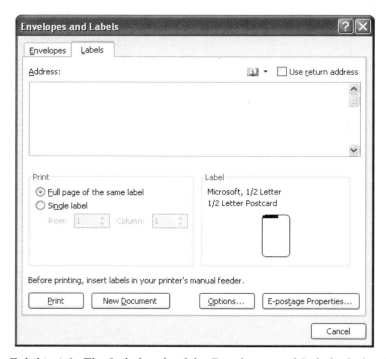

Exhibit 4-1: The Labels tab of the Envelopes and Labels dialog box

Inserting an address from Outlook

If you have address data stored in your Microsoft Outlook address book, you can insert it in the Envelopes and Labels dialog box. You can insert Outlook address data for an envelope or a label. To insert an address in the Envelopes and Labels dialog box:

1　Click the Insert Address button to open the Select Name dialog box.

2　Specify the contact address you want to add.

3　Click OK.

Do it!

A-1: Printing multiple labels for a single address

Here's how	Here's why
1 Create a new, blank document	Click the Office button and choose New. In the New Document dialog box, click Create.
2 Activate the Mailings tab	You often send packages to an associate in Phoenix, so you'll print a page of labels with her address on them.
In the Create group, click **Labels**	To open the Envelopes and Labels dialog box with the Labels tab activated.
3 Click **Options**	To open the Label Options dialog box.
From the Label vendors list, select **Avery US Letter**	If necessary.
From the Product number list, select **5160**	
Click **OK**	To close the Label Options dialog box and return to the Envelopes and Labels dialog box.
4 In the Address box, type **Southwestern Style Magazine**	
Press ⏎ ENTER	To create a line break.
5 Type **112 Rancho Blvd**	
Press ⏎ ENTER	
6 Type **Phoenix, AZ 85005**	
Press ⏎ ENTER	
7 Type **Attn: Christina Lanz**	
8 Under Print, verify that "Full page of the same label" is selected	
9 Click **New Document**	To create a document with the label settings you selected.
10 If your computer is connected to a printer, click	
Choose **Print**, **Quick Print**	To print the labels.

11 Save the document as **My labels**   Save the file in the current unit folder.

Close the file

Topic B: Envelopes

This topic covers the following Microsoft Certified Application Specialist exam objective for Word 2007.

#	Objective
4.5.3	**Create envelopes and labels**
	• Create a single envelope or label

Printing an envelope for a single recipient

Explanation

You can print single envelopes by using the Envelopes tab in the Envelopes and Labels dialog box. You can specify both the delivery and return addresses. If the current document is the letter you plan to send, then you might want to add the envelope as a page in the current document. In this way, you'll be able to print an envelope and the letter itself from the same document, and you won't need to use the Envelopes and Labels dialog box to generate the envelope in the future.

To print a single envelope:

1 Open or create a document.

2 Activate the Mailings tab.

3 In the Create group, click Envelope to open the Envelopes and Labels dialog box with the Envelopes tab activated, as shown in Exhibit 4-2.

4 Click Options to open the Envelope Options dialog box. Specify envelope and printing options, and click OK.

5 Under Delivery address and Return address (in the Envelopes and Labels dialog box), enter the appropriate addresses.

6 Click Print to print the document, or click New Document to generate a new document based on the settings you've specified.

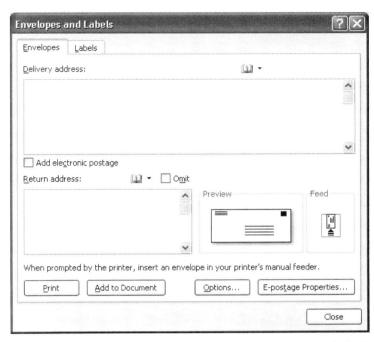

Exhibit 4-2: The Envelopes tab of the Envelopes and Labels dialog box

Do it!

B-1: Printing a single envelope

Here's how	Here's why
1 Create a new, blank document	If necessary.
2 Activate the Mailings tab	If necessary.
In the Create group, click **Envelopes**	To open the Envelopes and Labels dialog box with the Envelopes tab activated.
3 Click **Options**	To open the Envelope Options dialog box.
4 In the Envelope size list, verify that Size 10 is selected	
Click **OK**	To close the Envelope Options dialog box and return to the Envelopes and Labels dialog box.
5 In the Delivery Address box, type **Southwestern Style Magazine**	
Press (↵ ENTER)	
6 Type the following lines, pressing (↵ ENTER) after each line: **112 Rancho Blvd** **Phoenix, AZ 85005** **Attn: Christina Lanz**	You won't enter a return address because you have envelopes with your return address printed on them.
7 Click **Add to Document**	To add the envelope as a page in the current document, where you can edit it.
8 If you have a printer, click	
Choose **Print**, **Quick Print**	
9 Save the document as **My envelope**	
10 Close the document	

Unit summary: Printing labels and envelopes

Topic E   In this topic, you used the Envelopes and Labels dialog box to prepare and print a single address on every label on a sheet of **labels**.

Topic F   In this topic, you used the Envelopes and Labels dialog box to prepare and print an address on a single **envelope**.

Independent practice activity

In this activity, you'll specify a mailing address to print on a single label. You'll also specify a mailing address to print on an envelope.

1 Create a single mailing label that uses the 2163-Shipping label size.

2 For the label, specify the following address:
   Daniel Hanson
   Hanson Distributors
   631 Industrial Pkwy
   El Paso, TX 79909

3 Specify that you will print a single label.

4 Print the label, or click **Cancel**.

5 Create an envelope that uses the following delivery address:
   MK Franz
   MKF Fields
   18 Franklin St
   Frederick, MD 21704

6 Specify the following return address:
   Terry Park
   Outlander Spices
   28 Spice Way
   Portland, OR 97201

7 Verify that the addresses will print to a size 10 envelope. (*Hint*: Use the Envelope Options dialog box.)

8 Add the envelope to the current document. Do **not** save the return address as the default.

9 Save the file as **My practice envelope**.

10 Close all documents.

Review questions

1   In the Envelopes and Labels dialog box, how do you specify a label or envelope size?

2   After you create a label, what are the two printing choices available?

3   What is the advantage of adding an envelope to a document?

4   When you use the Envelopes and Labels dialog box to print addresses on envelopes, you must enter a return address. True or false?

5   How do you quickly create a label or envelope for an Outlook contact?

Unit 5

Templates and building blocks

Unit time: 30 minutes

Complete this unit, and you'll know how to:

A Create a document from a template, save and use your own template, and use the Templates folder to store a custom template.

B Use the Building Blocks Organizer to work with commonly used document elements.

C Use the Restrict Formatting and Editing pane to protect a document with a password, and view and edit document properties.

Topic A: Template basics

This topic covers the following Microsoft Certified Application Specialist exam objectives for Word 2007.

#	Objective
1.1.1	**Work with templates**
	• Create documents from templates (This objective is also covered in *Word 2007: Basic*, in the unit titled "Getting started.")
	• Create templates from documents
6.1.1	**Save to appropriate formats**
	• Save as a .doc, .docx, .xps, .docm, or .dotx file (This objective is also covered in *Word 2007: Basic*, in the unit titled "Getting started" and in *Word 2007: Advanced*, in the unit titled "Forms.")

Using templates to create documents

Explanation

Templates are pre-designed documents that contain formatting and, in some cases, boilerplate text or placeholder text. Templates are designed so that you can use them as the basis for documents you use often—such as memos, faxes, and letters—without having to spend a lot of time formatting them each time.

Word supplies many templates you can use to create documents. In fact, every time you create a document, you're using a template; Word bases new, blank documents on the Normal template. A new document's settings are all specified by the template settings. However, you can modify a template to change its default settings.

To use a template:

1   Click the Office button and choose New to open the New Document dialog box.

2   A list of template categories is displayed on the left side of the dialog box:

   • The active category is Blank and recent. It contains the Blank document template.

   • Click Installed Templates to see a list of templates stored locally on your computer.

   • Categories of online templates are listed under Microsoft Office Online.

3   Click a category name to see a corresponding gallery of templates. For example, if you want to create a memo, click Memos, and select one of the templates shown in Exhibit 5-1.

4   Select the template you want to use.

5   Click Create to use a template that's stored locally, or click Download to use an online template.

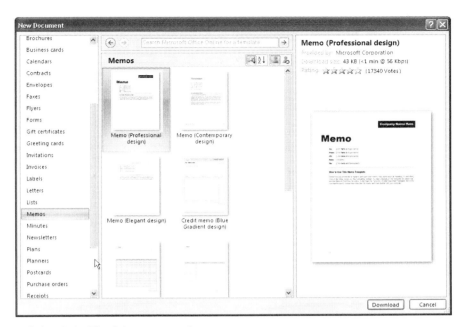

Exhibit 5-1: The Memos template category

A-1:   Using a template

Here's how	Here's why
1 Click	
Choose **New**	To open the New Document dialog box.
2 In the left pane, click several of the categories	To examine the templates in each category.
3 Select **Memos**	You might need to scroll down.
In the template pane, select **Memo (Professional design)**	If necessary.
Click **Download**	To create a document using the selected template. Word provides fields that contain prompts for information for the memo.
Click **Continue**	If necessary, to validate your version of Microsoft Word.
4 Save the document as **My memo**	In the current unit folder. (If a dialog box asks about format and compatibility, click OK.)
5 Click the To field, as shown	**To:** [Click here and type name] **From:** [Click here and type name]
	To select it.
Enter **Cedric Stone**	
Click the From field	
Enter **Ann Salinski**	
6 Remove the CC line from the document	Drag to select it and press Delete.
In the Re field, enter **New Kiosk Locations**	Click the Re field and type the text.
7 Select the text **Company Name Here**	Located in the top-right corner of the memo.
Enter **Outlander Spices**	To replace the text.
8 Update and close the document	

Creating templates

Explanation

When you create a document from a template, you don't actually edit the original template. Instead, Word creates a copy of the template. But you can also save a document as a template; you can create templates that include the text, graphics, tables, and objects of your choice. When you save a file as a template, it's saved in the .dotx file format.

To save a document as a template:

1 Create a new blank document, open an existing document, or create a new document from a template.

2 Enter or edit the text and apply the formatting that you want the template to contain.

3 Insert any tables, objects, or pictures that you want the template to contain.

4 Click the Office button and choose Save As.

5 From the Save as type list, select Word Template.

6 In the File name box, enter a name for the template.

7 Click Save to save the file as a template in the .dotx format.

Do it!

A-2:   Saving an altered template

Here's how	Here's why
1 Open the New Document dialog box	Click the Office button and choose New.
2 From the list of categories, select **Faxes**	
From the list of templates, select **Fax cover sheet (Professional design)**	If necessary.
Click **Download**	You will enter information on the cover sheet and then save the altered document as a new template.
3 In the top-right corner of the document, click **Company Name**	
Enter **Outlander Spices**	
4 In the Street Address field, enter **1150 Grant Street**	In the top-left corner of the document.
In the City, ST Zip Code field, enter **San Francisco, CA 94113**	
In the phone field, enter **415-969-9900**	
In the fax field, enter **415-969-9909**	
Remove the Web address field	
5 Click	
Choose **Save As**	To open the Save As dialog box.
6 In the File name box, enter **Outlander fax cover**	
From the Save as type list, select **Word Template**	
Save the document in the current unit folder	Click OK if a file format dialog box appears.
7 Close the document	

Using your own templates

Explanation   After you've created a template, you can create a document from it, just as you would with one of Word's built-in templates. However, your own templates don't show up in the categories listed in the New Document dialog box. To use your own templates (if they're not stored in Word's Templates folder):

1   Open the New Document dialog box.
2   Click "New from existing" to open the New from Existing Document dialog box.
3   Select the template you want to use.
4   Click Create New.

Do it!   ### A-3:   Creating a document from a user-defined template

Here's how	Here's why
1 Open the New Document dialog box	Click the Office button and choose New.
2 From the list of categories, select **New from existing...**	
3 Navigate to the current unit folder	If necessary.
Select **Outlander fax cover**	
Click **Create New**	To create a document based on this template. Notice that the document was given a generic file name, rather than the name of the template.
4 Close the document without updating it	

Using the Templates folder

Explanation

If you create your own templates and plan to use them frequently, it's a good idea to store them in Word's Templates folder. That way, you won't have to search for them whenever you want to use them. To use a custom template that you've stored in Word's Templates folder:

1   Open the New Document dialog box.

2   Click My templates to open the New dialog box, shown in Exhibit 5-2.

3   Select the template you want to use.

4   Click OK.

To save a template in Word's Templates folder, navigate to the folder's default location, which is C:\Documents and Settings\[user]\Application Data\Microsoft\Templates. (You have to be viewing hidden files in order to see this folder.)

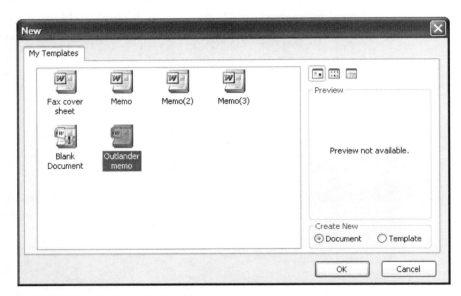

Exhibit 5-2: The New dialog box

Do it!   **A-4:   Saving a template in the Templates folder**

Here's how	Here's why
1 Open Memo	(From the current unit folder.) You will save this document as a template in the Templates folder so that it will be readily available whenever you use Microsoft Word.
2 Open the Save As dialog box	Click the Office button and choose Save As.
From the Save as type list, select **Word Template**	
Edit the File name box to read **Outlander memo**	
3 Navigate to the following folder: C:\Documents and Settings\[user]\Application Data\Microsoft\Templates	
Click **Save**	
4 Close the document	
5 Open the New Document dialog box	
From the list of categories, select **My templates...**	To open the New dialog box.
Select **Outlander memo**	
Click **OK**	To create a document using the template.
6 Close all open documents without updating	

Topic B: Building blocks

This topic covers the following Microsoft Certified Application Specialist exam objectives for Word 2007.

#	Objective
4.1.1	**Insert building blocks in documents**
	• Insert sidebars using the Building Blocks Organizer
	• Edit the properties of building block elements
	• Sort building blocks by name, gallery, or category
4.1.2	**Save frequently used data as building blocks**
	• Save company names or logos as building blocks
	• Save company contact information as building blocks
	• Modify and save building blocks with the same name
4.1.3	**Insert formatted headers and footers from Quick Parts**
	• Insert headers from Quick Parts and edit document titles

Working with building blocks

Explanation

A *building block* is a predefined portion of content—such as a cover page, header, or footer—that can be reused. Word 2007 provides a set of commonly used building blocks, organized in galleries. For example, the Cover Pages gallery contains all the cover-page building blocks. When you select a cover page from the gallery, it's already formatted with a certain look. It's automatically placed at the beginning of your document, and it contains placeholders, such as "[Type the document title]," indicating where you can enter your text. By using building blocks, you can create documents much more quickly.

Building blocks also provide a cohesive look for your documents. For example, the Cover Pages, Headers, and Footers galleries each contain a building block named Alphabet. Each one incorporates the same color scheme and fonts, among other attributes. By using all three of these building blocks, you create a document whose cover page, headers, and footers all have a consistent style.

The Building Blocks Organizer

You can access all building blocks, from all galleries, in the Building Blocks Organizer, shown in Exhibit 5-3. To open the Building Blocks Organizer:

1   Activate the Insert tab.

2   In the Text group, click Quick Parts.

3   Choose Building Blocks Organizer.

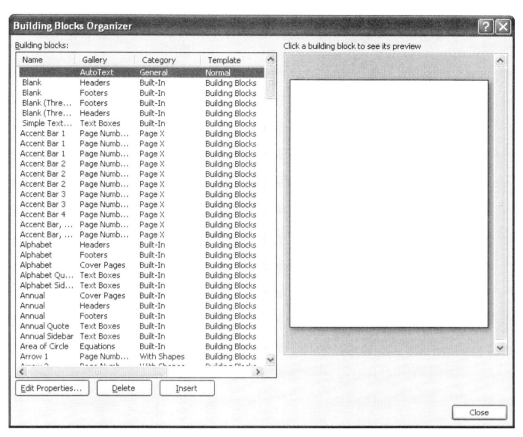

Exhibit 5-3: The Building Blocks Organizer

Each building block is associated with a name, gallery, category, template, behavior, and description. To find a building block more quickly, you can sort the list displayed in the Building Block Organizer. To do so, click the heading of the column by which you'd like to sort.

For example, if you know the name of the building block you want to use, click the Name column heading to sort alphabetically by building block name. Or, if you know you'd like a cover page, but you're not sure which style, click the Gallery column heading to see all the cover-page building blocks arranged together.

Do it!   ## B-1:   Using the Building Blocks Organizer

Here's how	Here's why
1 Create a new blank document	You'll experiment with building blocks.
2 Activate the Insert tab	
3 In the Text group, click **Quick Parts**	
Choose **Building Blocks Organizer...**	To open the Building Blocks Organizer dialog box.
4 Click the Name column heading	(If necessary.) To sort the list alphabetically by building block name.
5 In the Building blocks list, locate the Alphabet building blocks	There are several building blocks with this name, but each one is a different document component, located in a different gallery.
Observe the Gallery column	There are Alphabet building blocks in the Headers, Footers, and Cover Pages galleries.
Select **Alphabet**	(From any gallery.) Notice the preview displayed on the right. Below the preview is a description of the document element.
6 Click the Gallery column heading	To sort the building blocks by Gallery name.
Scroll the building block list	There are galleries of bibliographies, cover pages, equations, footers, headers, text boxes, and more.
Click the Name column heading	To sort building blocks by name.

Adding a building block to a document

Explanation

The Building Block Organizer lists many building blocks. In addition to cover pages, headers, and footers, there are also sidebars. A *sidebar* is a formatted text box that appears along the side of a document page.

To insert a building block, such as a sidebar, in a document:

1   Activate the Insert tab.
2   In the Text group, click Quick Parts, and choose Building Blocks Organizer.
3   From the Building blocks list, select the desired building block.
4   Click Insert.

After you add a building block to your document, you can edit its properties. When you add a sidebar, the Text Box Tools appear, adding a Format tab to the Ribbon. You can use the tools available on this tab to further customize the sidebar.

Inserting a header from Quick Parts

If you'd like to add a header to a document, sort the list in the Building Blocks Organizer alphabetically by gallery. This places all the building blocks in the Headers gallery together in the list, making them easy to find. Scroll the list of building blocks to view the headers. Select the desired header and click Insert.

After adding the header building block, you can use the placeholders, called *content controls*, to customize it with your information. For example, you can click the [Type the document title] content control and enter your document's title.

Do it!

B-2: Inserting building blocks

Here's how	Here's why
1 Verify that the Building Blocks Organizer dialog box is open	If necessary, on the Insert tab, in the Text group, click Quick Parts and choose Building Blocks Organizer.
From the Building blocks list, select **Annual Sidebar**	
Click **Insert**	To add this building block to the document. The Text Box Tools appear, adding a Format tab to the Ribbon.
2 Save the document as **My report**	In the current unit folder.
3 On the Format tab, click **3-D Effects**	
Click **3-D Effects**	To display a gallery of three-dimensional effects that can be applied to the sidebar.
Under Parallel, select 3-D Style 1, as shown	
	To apply this 3-D style to the sidebar.
4 In the Arrange group, click **Position**	To display the gallery of position options.
Under With Text Wrapping, select the indicated option	
	(Position in Top Left with Square Text Wrapping.) To position the sidebar on the left side of the page.
5 Open the Building Blocks Organizer dialog box	Activate the Insert tab. In the Text group, click Quick Parts and choose Building Blocks Organizer.

6 Enter **p**

To move to the building blocks whose names begin with the letter P. You want to select a header named Pinstripes.

Select **Pinstripes**

Pinstripes	Cover Pages
Pinstripes	Footers
Pinstripes	Headers
Pinstripes Q...	Text Boxes

Verify that you've selected the Pinstripes building block from the Headers gallery.

Click **Insert**

To add the header to the document.

7 In the header, click
Type the document title

To select the content control.

Enter **Company Report**

Title
Company Report

8 Update the file

Creating your own building blocks

Explanation

You might want to create your own building blocks and store them in the Building Blocks Organizer. For example, if you have a company logo and contact information that you'll often need to include in documents, you'll want to store them as building blocks. That way, you won't have to re-create these elements each time you want to use them.

To create your own building block:

1 In your document, select the element (such as a company logo or address) that you want to save as a building block.

2 On the Insert tab, click Quick Parts, and choose Save Selection to Quick Part Gallery. This opens the Create New Building Block dialog box, shown in Exhibit 5-4.

3 In the Name box, enter a name for the building block.

4 From the Gallery list, select the gallery where you want to store the building block.

5 From the Category list, select a category for the building block. If you want to add a new category, select Create New Category from the list.

6 In the Description box, enter any clarifying information about the building block.

7 From the Save in list, select the template in which to save the building block.

8 In the Options list, specify whether to include content only, or include breaks to place content in its own paragraph or on its own page.

9 Click OK.

Exhibit 5-4: The Create New Building Block dialog box

Do it!

B-3: Creating building blocks

Here's how	Here's why
1 Open Building blocks	From the current unit folder.
2 Click **Outlander Spices**	(At the top of the page.) To select this graphic element. You'll save this as a building block so that it can easily be used in other documents.
3 Activate the Insert tab	

4 In the Text group, click
   Quick Parts

   Choose **Save Selection to**   To open the Create New Building Block dialog
   Quick Part Gallery...   box.

5 In the Name box, enter   To name the building block.
   Outlander graphic

   From the Options list, select
   Insert content in its own paragraph

   Click **OK**   To save this graphic element as a building block.

6 Drag to select the company
   contact information, as shown

   | 1150 Grant Street |
   | San Francisco, CA 94113 |
   | Phone: (415) 969-9900 |
   | Fax: (415) 969-9909 |

   You'll save this as a building block as well.

7 Open the Create New Building   Click Quick Parts and choose Save Selection to
   Block dialog box   Quick Part Gallery.

   In the Name box, enter   To name the building block.
   Outlander contact info

   From the Options list, select
   Insert content in its own paragraph

   Click **OK**   To create the building block.

8 Close Building blocks   If prompted, don't save changes.

9 Double-click in My report   To place the insertion point in the document
                                                itself, not in the header or the sidebar.

10 Open the Building Blocks
   Organizer dialog box

11 Move to the building blocks   Enter O.
   whose names begin with the letter
   "O"

   Select **Outlander g...**   To select the Outlander graphic.

   Click **Insert**   To add the Outlander graphic to the report.

12 Press ⏎ ENTER   To create a new line in the report.

Altering building blocks

Explanation

After you create a building block, you might want to modify it. For example, perhaps your company logo or address needs to be updated. To modify a building block:

1 In your document, select the updated building block.

2 On the Insert tab, click Quick Parts and choose Save Selection to Quick Part Gallery to open the Create New Building Block dialog box.

3 In the Name box, enter the same name you previously assigned to the building block.

4 Specify the remaining options in the dialog box as desired.

5 Click OK. A message box asks if you'd like to redefine the previous building block entry.

6 Click Yes to replace the previous building block with the updated one.

Do it!   **B-4:   Modifying a building block**

Here's how	Here's why
1 Add the Outlander contact info building block to the document	Open the Building Blocks Organizer, select Outlander c…, and click Insert.
2 Edit the street address to read **1150 Main Street**	To change the street name from Grant Street to Main Street.
3 Select the company contact information, as shown	1150 Main Street San Francisco, CA 94113 Phone: (415) 969-9900 Fax: (415) 969-9909
4 Click **Quick Parts** Choose **Save Selection to Quick Part Gallery…**	
5 In the Name box, enter **Outlander contact info**	This is the same name used to originally save this building block.
From the Options list, select **Insert content in its own paragraph**	
Click **OK**	A message box appears, asking if you'd like to redefine the building block entry.
6 Click **Yes**	To replace the old building block with this updated version.
Update and close the document	
7 Create a new blank document	
8 Insert the Outlander contact info building block	On the Insert tab, click Quick Parts. Choose Building Blocks Organizer, select Outlander c…, and click Insert.
Observe the street address	The street name should be updated to Main Street.

Removing a building block

Explanation

If a building block becomes obsolete, you can remove it. To delete a building block:

1 Open the Building Blocks Organizer dialog box.
2 From the Building blocks list, select the building block you want to delete.
3 Click Yes to confirm the deletion.
4 Click Close to close the Building Blocks Organizer dialog box.

Do it!

B-5: Deleting building blocks

Here's how	Here's why
1 Open the Building Blocks Organizer dialog box	
2 From the Building blocks list, select **Outlander c...**	To select the Outlander contact info building block.
3 Click **Delete**	A message box appears, asking you to confirm that you'd like to delete the selected building block.
Click **Yes**	To delete the building block.
4 Verify that Outlander graphic is selected	It's automatically selected because it's next in the list.
5 Click **Delete**	
Click **Yes**	To delete the Outlander graphic building block.
6 Click **Close**	To close the Building Blocks Organizer.
Close the document	Don't save changes.

Topic C: Document properties

This topic covers the following Microsoft Certified Application Specialist exam objectives for Word 2007.

#	Objective
1.3.3	**Modify document properties** • Add key words
6.2.1	**Restrict permissions to documents** (This objective is also covered in *Word 2007: Advanced*, in the unit titled "Forms.")
6.2.3	**Set passwords** (This objective is also covered in *Word 2007: Advanced*, in the unit titled "Forms.")
6.2.4	**Protect documents** • Set editing restrictions (This objective is also covered in the unit titled "Managing document revisions" and in *Word 2007: Advanced*, in the unit titled "Forms.")

Protecting documents

Explanation

After you've created a document, you might want to protect it so that others can't change something without authorization. You can assign a password to the document to protect it, and you can specify which kinds of changes you will allow people to make. In addition, you can view and edit document properties. These provide more information and can provide added security.

You can protect documents by setting editing and formatting restrictions and by assigning passwords to them. Two types of restrictions can be assigned:

- *Formatting restrictions* prevent someone from modifying or using styles that you specify. This can effectively prevent other people from applying any formatting to a document.

- *Editing restrictions* let you select the kind of editing allowed in a document: Tracked Changes, Comments, Filling in forms, or No changes (Read only).

To protect a document:

1 On the Review tab, in the Protect group, click Protect Document to open the Restrict Formatting and Editing task pane, shown in Exhibit 5-5.

2 Under Formatting restrictions, check the box to limit formatting to a selection of styles. Then click Settings to open the Formatting Restrictions dialog box. Select the desired options and click OK.

3 Under Editing restrictions, check the box to apply editing restrictions; then select an option from the list.

4 Under Start Enforcement, click "Yes, Start Enforcing Protection" to open the Start Enforcing Protection dialog box.

5 Enter a password; then re-enter it to confirm it.

6 Click OK.

After a document is protected, you can remove protection by clicking Stop Protection in the Restrict Formatting and Editing pane. When you do, the Unprotect Document dialog box will open, and you can enter the password.

Exhibit 5-5: The Restrict Formatting and Editing pane

Password guidelines

When creating passwords, follow these guidelines:

- Passwords are case sensitive.
- Passwords can contain up to 15 characters.
- Any combination of letters, numerals, spaces, and symbols can be used.
- Including capital letters and numbers creates stronger passwords.
- Be sure to remember the password. Lost passwords cannot be recovered.

Do it!

C-1: Protecting a document

Here's how	Here's why
1 Open Spice info	From the current unit folder.
Save the document as **My spice info**	In the current unit folder.
2 Activate the Review tab	
In the Protect group, click **Protect Document**	To open the Restrict Formatting and Editing pane.
3 Under Editing restrictions, check the check box	You will leave the list set to "No changes (Read only)" to make the document read-only.
Under Start enforcement, click **Yes, Start Enforcing Protection**	To open the Start Enforcing Protection dialog box.
4 In the "Enter new password (optional)" box, enter **password**	
In the "Reenter password to confirm" box, enter **password**	
Click **OK**	To close the dialog box.
5 Attempt to edit the document	The document is read-only. In the Restrict Formatting and Editing pane, a message indicates that you can't modify the document.
6 In the Restrict Formatting and Editing pane, click **Stop Protection**	To open the Unprotect Document dialog box.
In the Password box, enter **password**	
Click **OK**	To close the dialog box.
7 Edit the document	You can now make changes.
Press $\boxed{CTRL}$ + $\boxed{Z}$	To undo your change.
8 Update the document	
Close the Restrict Formatting and Editing pane	

Editing document properties

Explanation

You can view and edit a document's properties by clicking the Office button and choosing Prepare, Properties. These properties are also sometimes referred to as *metadata*. The document's properties appear below the Ribbon in the Document Information Panel, shown in Exhibit 5-6. The panel provides a variety of information about the document or template. Enter information in the boxes to save that information as part of the document. You can then easily organize and identify your documents later based on this information.

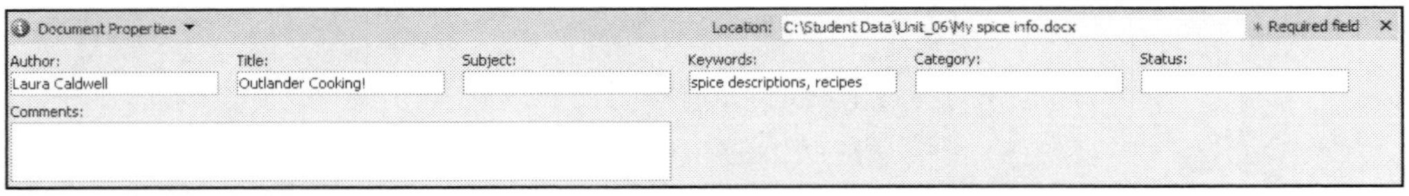

Document Properties ▼			Location: C:\Student Data\Unit_06\My spice info.docx		* Required field ✕
Author:	Title:	Subject:	Keywords:	Category:	Status:
Laura Caldwell	Outlander Cooking!		spice descriptions, recipes		
Comments:					

Exhibit 5-6: The Document Information Panel

Do it!

C-2: Viewing and editing document properties

Here's how	Here's why
1 Click	
Choose **Prepare**, **Properties**	To display the document properties.
2 In the Author box, enter **Laura Caldwell**	
In the Title box, enter **Outlander Cooking!**	
In the Keywords box, enter **spice descriptions, recipes**	
3 Update and close the document	
4 Click	
Choose **Open**	
5 From the list of files, select **My spice info**	
Click as shown	(The Views button in the upper-right corner of the Open dialog box.) To display a menu of view options.
Choose **Properties**	To display the properties of the selected file.
6 Observe the document properties	If you're searching for documents with spice descriptions or recipes, you can tell by examining the Keywords property that this document might be of interest.
Click **Open**	To open the My spice info file.

Document statistics

Explanation

To quickly view some statistics about a document, click the Words section on the left side of the status bar. This opens the Word Count dialog box, shown in Exhibit 5-7. The dialog box shows information about the text in the document.

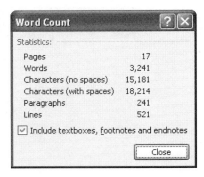

Exhibit 5-7: Document statistics

To view more statistics about the document, including the date it was created and modified, open the <Document> Properties dialog box, shown in Exhibit 5-8. From the Document Properties list (in the upper-left corner of the Document Information Panel), choose Advanced Properties.

Exhibit 5-8: Advanced document properties

Do it!   ## C-3:   Viewing document statistics

Here's how	Here's why
1 Click as shown	 Document Properties ▾
Choose **Advanced Properties...**	To open the Properties dialog box for the current document.
2 Activate the Statistics tab	To view document statistics.
3 Click **Cancel**	To return to the document.
4 Close the document properties	
Update and close the document	

Unit summary: Templates and building blocks

Topic A   In this topic, you used the New Document dialog box to create a document from a **template**. Then you saved and used your own template, and you learned how to use the Templates folder to store a custom template.

Topic B   In this topic, you used the **Building Blocks Organizer** to insert a sidebar and header in a document. You also created your own building blocks for a company graphic and contact information. Finally, you modified and deleted building blocks.

Topic C   In this topic, you used the Restrict Formatting and Editing pane to **protect** a document with a password. Then you viewed and edited document **properties**. You also learned how to view a document's **statistics**.

Independent practice activity

In this activity, you'll create a document from a template. Then you'll edit the document and save it as a new template in Word's Templates folder. Next, you'll enable password protection for a document and edit its properties.

1 Create a document from the Formal Meeting Minutes template, located in the Minutes template category.

2 Edit the Company/Department Name field to read **Outlander Spices: Marketing**.

3 Save the document as a template named **My practice minutes** in Word's Templates folder. (*Hint*: Word's Template folder is C:\Documents and Settings\[user]\ Application Data\Microsoft\Templates.)

4 Close the document.

5 Open Practice properties (from the current unit folder), and save it as **My practice properties**.

6 Protect the document so that no changes are allowed without the password "password."

7 Show the document properties.

8 In the Author field, enter your name.

9 View the statistics for the document.

10 Close the document properties and the Restrict Formatting and Editing pane.

11 Update and close the document.

Review questions

1 When you create a Word document, which template is used by default?

2 What are the steps for creating a document based on a template?

3 Where should you save a template you've created or customized so that it is easily accessible from the New Document dialog box?

4 Which of the following statements about building blocks is false?

    A Examples of building blocks include predefined headers, footers, and cover pages.

    B To open the Building Blocks Organizer dialog box, activate the Insert tab; then, in the Text group, click Building Blocks Organizer.

    C A building block is a predefined portion of content.

    D Building blocks can provide a cohesive look for your documents.

5 Where can you set a password to protect a document from unwanted edits?

    A The Restrict Formatting and Editing pane

    B The Properties pane

    C The Application Settings dialog box

    D The Password group

6 The Word Count dialog box shows all of the following information about a document, except:

    A Pages

    B Words

    C Paragraphs

    D Author

Unit 6

Graphics

Unit time: 45 minutes

Complete this unit, and you'll know how to:

A Create and modify a diagram.

B Insert text boxes and shapes in a document, and modify them by adjusting their size, shape, and other attributes.

C Format text graphically, using WordArt, drop caps, and pull quotes.

Topic A: Diagrams

This topic covers the following Microsoft Certified Application Specialist exam objectives for Word 2007.

#	Objective
3.1.1	**Insert SmartArt graphics**
3.2.3	**Apply Quick Styles**
3.2.5	**Add text to SmartArt graphics and shapes** (This objective is also covered in Topic B.)

Creating diagrams using SmartArt graphics

Explanation

You can use Word to create diagrams, such as organization charts, that visually represent relationships or processes.

You can insert a diagram by using the Choose a SmartArt Graphic dialog box, shown in Exhibit 6-1. You can choose from some commonly used standard diagrams, such as process, cycle, or hierarchy diagrams.

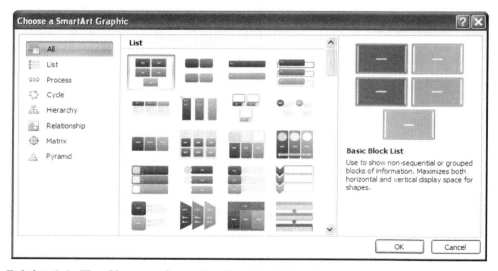

Exhibit 6-1: The Choose a SmartArt Graphic dialog box

The Choose a SmartArt Graphic dialog box divides the diagrams into categories, which are described in the following table.

Diagram	Illustrates
List	Groups of information, which can be sequential (following a progression) or non-sequential.
Process	Steps leading toward a goal. For example, use this diagram to show the steps involved in hiring a new employee.
Cycle	The steps of a cyclical process. For example, use this diagram to describe the process of developing a product, marketing it, and reinvesting profit in further development.
Hierarchy	The hierarchical relationships among elements. For example, use an organization chart to represent the positions in a corporation.
Relationship	The relationships among items. For example, use a Venn diagram to show company resources used by two departments, differentiating among shared resources and resources used only in a given department.
Matrix	The relationship of different components to a whole.
Pyramid	Containment, overlapping, proportional, or interconnected relationships between components.

To insert a diagram into a document:

1   Place the insertion point where you want to insert the diagram.
2   Activate the Insert tab.
3   In the Illustrations group, click SmartArt to open the Choose a SmartArt Graphic dialog box.
4   On the left, select a diagram type.
5   From the list of diagrams in that category, select the specific diagram you want.
6   Click OK to insert the diagram on a *drawing canvas* (the space in which you work on graphics or drawings). The Text pane appears, containing the diagram's placeholder text.
7   Click a text placeholder, and type the text you want to display in the diagram.

When you insert or work with SmartArt graphics, Word displays a set of SmartArt Tools. These tools are on two additional Ribbon tabs: Design and Format.

Adding text to a SmartArt graphic

After your SmartArt graphic is inserted in a document, you can add text to it by using the Text pane. To show this pane, select the SmartArt graphic. Then, on the Design tab, in the Create Graphic group, click Text Pane. (You can also click the control icon on the left edge of the frame that appears around the graphic when it's selected.) To hide this pane, click Text Pane again.

Do it! **A-1:   Creating an organization chart**

Here's how	Here's why
1 Create a new, blank document	
Save the document as **My org chart**	In the current unit folder.
2 Activate the Insert tab	
In the Illustrations group, click **SmartArt**	To open the Choose a SmartArt Graphic dialog box.
3 On the left, select **Hierarchy**	To select the Hierarchy category of graphics.
Click	(The Hierarchy option.) To select the type of chart you'd like to create.
Click **OK**	To insert the organization chart on the page.
4 Click as shown	(If necessary.) To show the Text pane.
5 In the Text pane, under "Type your text here," click the first bullet	(If necessary.) To select it so you can enter custom text.
6 Enter **VP Global Sales**	Notice that the top box of the organization chart contains the text you typed.
7 Click the second bullet point	(In the Text pane.) This bullet is subordinate to the first, so the box is located in the second row of the chart, with a connecting line between the two boxes.
Enter **Director North American Sales**	As you type, the text is automatically aligned and sized within the box.
8 Press ⏎ ENTER	To create another bullet point at the same level as the previous one. A new box is created on the second row.
Enter **Director Global Sales**	

9 Press `↵ ENTER`	To create another bullet point.
Press `TAB`	To demote the bullet point to the third level.
Enter **Director European Sales**	
Create another third-level bullet point	Press Enter.
Enter **Director Pacific Rim Sales**	

You will now remove the bullet points you don't need.

10 Point to the [Text] bullet below the one you just added	
Drag down to select the remaining [Text] bullet points	
11 Press `← BACKSPACE`	

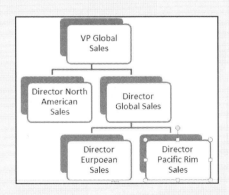

To remove the extra boxes from the chart.

12 Update the document

Formatting diagrams

Explanation

When you select a diagram, a border appears around it, and the SmartArt Tools appear, adding a Design tab and a Format tab to the Ribbon. You can use these tabs to modify the layout and formatting of your diagram. Use the Design tab to change the diagram type or layout, change the diagram shapes, and apply Quick Styles to the diagram. Use the Format tab to modify and format individual diagram shapes and to format the diagram text.

Do it!

A-2: Formatting an organization chart

Here's how	Here's why
1 Verify that the organization chart is selected	A border appears around the chart when it is selected.
2 Observe the Ribbon	When a diagram is selected, the SmartArt Tools appear, adding Design and Format tabs to the Ribbon.
3 Under SmartArt Tools, activate the Design tab	(If necessary.) The Ribbon displays the diagram design settings.
4 In the SmartArt Styles group, click **Change Colors**	To display a color gallery.
Under Colorful, select the first option	(The Colorful - Accent Colors option.) To apply the color scheme to the chart.
5 In the SmartArt Styles group, click the More arrow, as shown	To display the SmartArt Styles gallery.
Under 3-D, select Inset, as shown	To apply the 3-D Inset style to the chart. Next, you'll use the Format tab to format individual objects in the organization chart.
6 Activate the Format tab	(On the SmartArt Tools tab.) You'll format the second-level shapes to use a different color.

7 In the Text pane, drag to select **Director North American Sales** and **Director Global Sales**, as shown

To select the corresponding shapes in the diagram.

8 In the Shape Styles group, click as shown

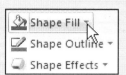

To open the Shape Fill gallery.

Click as shown

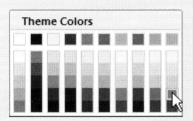

To select the Orange, Accent 6, Darker 25% color.

9 Update the document

Topic B: Drawing tools

This topic covers the following Microsoft Certified Application Specialist exam
objectives for Word 2007.

#	Objective
3.1.3	**Insert shapes**
3.2.5	**Add text to SmartArt graphics and shapes** (This objective is also covered in Topic A.)
3.4.1	**Insert text boxes**
3.4.2	**Format text boxes**
3.4.3	**Link text boxes**

Drawing shapes

Explanation

You can add a variety of shapes to a Word document. You can add basic geometric
shapes and symbols, lines, block arrows, flowchart symbols, callouts, stars, and banners.
A *callout* is used for labeling pictures or other graphics.

You can draw shapes by selecting a shape from the Shapes gallery, shown in Exhibit 6-
2. To expand the Shapes gallery, activate the Insert tab and click the More button in the
Shapes group. After selecting a shape, you can drag to draw it in the document. If you
press Shift while drawing a shape, it maintains its original proportions.

When you create or work with shapes, Word displays the Drawing Tools, adding a
Format tab to the Ribbon.

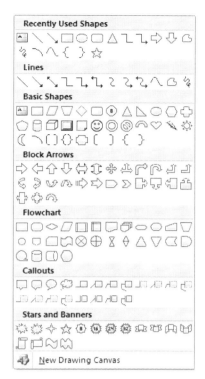

Exhibit 6-2: The Shapes gallery

B-1: Drawing a shape

Here's how	Here's why
1 Click outside the border around the diagram	To deselect the diagram.
2 Activate the Insert tab	
In the Illustrations group, click **Shapes**	To open the Shapes gallery.
Under Block Arrows, select the first arrow, as shown	
3 Position the pointer as shown	
Drag to the right as shown	
	To create an arrow.

Modifying shapes

Explanation

After creating a shape, you can modify it in a variety of ways. You can move, resize, reshape, or rotate it. In addition, you can specify a shape's fill and line attributes. When you edit a shape, the point from which you drag determines the type of editing you will perform.

Moving a shape

When you point inside a shape or along its edge, the pointer appears as a white arrow with a four-headed arrow at its tip, as shown in Exhibit 6-3. This pointer indicates that you can drag to move the shape. In addition, after you select a shape, you can press the arrow keys to nudge the shape in small increments for precise positioning.

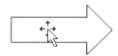

Exhibit 6-3: The pointer as it appears when placed within a shape

Resizing a shape

When you select a shape, *sizing handles* appear at each corner and along each edge of an imaginary rectangle around the shape. When you point to a sizing handle, the pointer appears as a two-headed arrow, as shown in Exhibit 6-4. Dragging a sizing handle resizes the shape:

- Drag a corner sizing handle to change the width and height.
- Drag a sizing handle along an edge to change only the height or the width.
- Press Shift while dragging a corner sizing handle to change the width and the height proportionally.

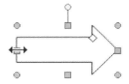

Exhibit 6-4: The pointer as it appears when placed on a sizing handle

Rotating a shape

When you select a shape, a green *rotate handle* appears above it. When you point to the rotate handle, the pointer appears as a circular arrow, as shown in Exhibit 6-5. You can drag the rotate handle to rotate the shape.

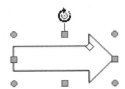

Exhibit 6-5: The pointer as it appears when placed on a rotate handle

Reshaping a shape

When you select a shape, it might display a yellow *adjustment handle*. You can drag an adjustment handle to reshape the shape. For example, with an arrow shape, you can change the thickness and length of the line part, change the size or shape of the arrowhead, or make the whole arrow short and thick or long and thin—to name just a few variations. When you point to an adjustment handle, the pointer appears as a white arrowhead, as shown in Exhibit 6-6.

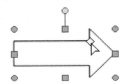

Exhibit 6-6: The pointer as it appears when placed on an adjustment handle

Adding text to a shape

You might want to modify a shape by adding text to it. To enter text within a shape, right-click inside the shape and choose Add Text. Then type the desired text.

Do it!

B-2: Modifying a shape

Here's how	Here's why
1 Point to the white area within the arrow shape	
	A four-headed arrow appears at the tip of the pointer, indicating that you can click to select the arrow shape or you can drag to move it.

2 Drag the arrow to position it as shown

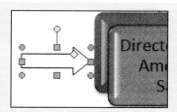

3 Press the arrow keys

To nudge the arrow shape in small increments. Next, you'll shorten the arrow shape.

4 Point to the left, middle sizing handle, as shown

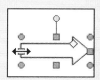

The pointer appears as a two-headed horizontal arrow, indicating that you can drag to change the shape's width.

Drag to the right

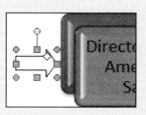

To shorten the arrow shape. Next, you'll rotate the arrow shape.

5 Point to the rotate handle, as shown

The pointer appears as a circular arrow, indicating that you can drag to rotate the shape.

Drag to the left

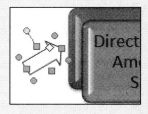

To rotate the arrow shape.

6 Press ⌈ CTRL ⌋ + ⌈ Z ⌋

To undo the rotation. Finally, you'll reshape the arrow.

7   Point to the yellow adjustment
    handle

    Drag the adjustment handle   To experiment with reshaping the arrow.

8   Press (CTRL) + (Z)   To undo the adjustment.

9   Open the Shapes gallery   In the Illustrations group, click Shapes.

    Under Stars and Banners, select
    the Wave shape, as shown

10 In the upper-right corner of the
    document, drag to create the wave
    shape

11 Right-click inside the shape   To display a shortcut menu.

    Choose **Add Text**

    Enter **Outlander Spices**

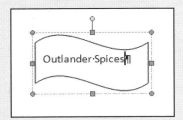

12 Drag to select the text

    Format the text as Trebuchet MS,   Use the Font group on the Home tab.
    10 pt, bold, centered

    Resize the shape   If necessary.

    Update the document

Using text boxes

Explanation

You can enter text inside a drawn object by using a text box. To draw a text box:

1 Activate the Insert tab.
2 In the Text group, click Text Box and choose Draw Text Box. The pointer changes to a large plus symbol.
3 Drag to specify the width and height of the text box, which is drawn as a rectangle or square.
4 Type to enter text in the text box.

If the text doesn't fit well, you can resize the text box by dragging any of its sizing handles.

When you create or work with text boxes, Word displays the Text Box Tools, adding a Format tab to the Ribbon.

Converting a shape to a text box

You can add text within any shape by converting that shape to a text box. To add text within an existing shape, you select the shape and do either of the following:

• On the Drawing Tools | Format tab, in the Insert Shapes group, click Add Text.
• Right-click the shape and choose Add Text.

The Drawing Tools will be replaced by Text Box Tools on the Ribbon.

Linking text boxes

If you have two or more text boxes, you can link them to allow text to flow continuously from one text box to the next. To link two text boxes:

1 Enter the text in one text box, and keep that text box selected.
2 In the Text group on the Format tab, click Create Link.
3 Click the empty text box where you want the text to be continued.

Do it!

B-3: Inserting a text box

Here's how	Here's why
1 Activate the Insert tab	
2 In the Text group, click **Text Box** and choose **Draw Text Box**	The pointer appears as a large plus sign, which you can drag to create a text box.
3 Drag to create a text box on the page, as shown	
	The insertion point is in the text box, so you can type the text.
	The Text Box Tools | Format tab appears on the Ribbon.
4 Enter **Four regional directors will be appointed in the next fiscal year**	The text box might not be large enough to display all of this text.
5 In the Text group, click **Draw Text Box**	On the Format tab.
Draw a second text box below the first one, as shown	
6 Select the first text box	Click the outside border of the text box.
In the Text group, click **Create Link**	The mouse pointer shape changes to a pitcher with a down-arrow.
Click the empty text box	To link the second, empty, text box with the first. The text from the first text box spills over into the second one.
7 Press CTRL + Z	To undo the link.
Delete the second text box	Click to select the text box border and then press Delete. You'll solve the text overflow problem by using another method.

Formatting text boxes

Explanation

You can format a text box and you can format the text within a text box. To select and format the text within a text box, use the same techniques you'd use to select and format text in a typical document.

When you select a text box, the Text Box Tools appear, adding a Format tab to the Ribbon. Use the Format tab to format the text box by selecting options from the groups described in the following table.

Group	Description
Text	Draw a text box, and change the direction that the text flows within the text box. Link and unlink text boxes to control how text flows among multiple text boxes.
Text Box Styles	Change the shape. Apply a fill to the text box by adding a shape fill, picture, texture, or gradient. Apply an outline (border) to the text box, and adjust the weight, or thickness, of the outline.
Shadow Effects	Specify a shadow style, color, and direction for the text box.
3-D Effects	Apply three-dimensional effects to a text box.
Arrange	Change a text box's horizontal or vertical position and text wrapping. If more than one text box is displayed, you can use this group to change the stacking order of the boxes.
Size	Change the height and width of a text box. You can also change its rotation and scale.

Do it!

B-4: Formatting a text box

Here's how	Here's why
1 Select the text box	
Press (CTRL) + (A)	To select the text within the box.
2 Format the text as Trebuchet MS, 9 point, centered	Use the Font group, located on the Home tab.
3 Resize the text box until it is just large enough to display all of the text	

(Drag the sizing handles.) Next, you'll change the text box's fill and outline.

4 With the text box selected, activate the Text Box Tools tab	The Text Box Tools tab appears only when a text box is selected.
In the Text Box Styles group, click **Shape Outline** and choose **No Outline**	To remove the visible border from the text box.
5 In the Text Box Styles group, in the Shape Fill gallery, click as shown	

To select a light blue color, Blue, Accent 1, Lighter 60%.

6 Update the document	

Arranging objects

Explanation

When you create multiple text boxes or shapes, you might need to change how the objects overlap one another or align with one another. You can arrange text boxes and shapes by using the tools on the Format tab. When you select a shape, the Drawing Tools tab appears on the Ribbon, and when you select a text box, the Text Box Tools tab appears on the Ribbon. Each of these tabs includes an Arrange group, which contains options for specifying how objects overlap and align with one another.

Stacking order

The order in which objects overlap is known as the *stacking order*. Newer shapes or text boxes you create will appear in front of older items if they overlap. To change the stacking order, select the item whose stacking order you want to change, and select an option from the Arrange group on the Format tab. You can click the Bring to Front or Send to Back buttons to move an object, or you can click either button's down-arrow to display a menu with additional options for adjusting the stacking order.

Alignment

To align shapes or text boxes with one another:

1   Select the items you want to align.
2   Activate the Format tab (under Drawing Tools or Text Box Tools on the Ribbon).
3   In the Arrange group, click Position and choose the type of alignment you want.

Do it!

B-5: Arranging multiple objects

Here's how	Here's why
1 Point to an edge of the text box and click	To select the text box so that the insertion point no longer appears in it.
2 Press $\rightarrow$ several times	
	To move the text box to the right so that it overlaps the arrow shape's left edge. The text box and arrow shape overlap, the text box appears on top because it was created more recently. You'll send the text box to the back so that the arrow shape appears in front of it.
3 In the Arrange group, click **Send to Back**	(Don't click the down-arrow.) To send the text box to the back of the stacking order. Clicking the down-arrow on the Send to Back button displays a menu with several stacking-order commands.
4 Click **Bring to Front**	To bring the text box back to the top of the stacking order.
5 Update the document	

Changing shapes into different shapes

Explanation

After creating a shape or text box, you can convert to a different shape. For example, after you create an arrow shape and apply formatting to it, you might decide to change to a different type of arrow (or a different shape altogether). If you delete the current shape and start over, you'll have to draw the new shape and reapply all the formatting you applied to the old shape. However, if you simply change the current shape, it will appear as the new shape but will retain any formatting you already applied.

To change one shape into another:

1 Select the shape.
2 Activate the Drawing Tools | Format tab.
3 In the Shape Styles group, click Change Shape to display the Shapes gallery.
4 Select the desired shape.

Changing a text box shape

To change the shape of an existing text box:

1 Select the text box.
2 Activate the Text Box Tools | Format tab.
3 In the Text Box Styles group, click Change Shape to display the Shapes gallery.
4 Select the desired shape.

B-6:   Changing a shape into another shape

Here's how	Here's why
1 Click a blank space	To deselect the two shapes.
2 Click the text box	The Text Box Tools will appear on the Ribbon.
3 Activate the Format tab	(If necessary.) You'll change the text box shape so that it stands out visually from the organization chart.
4 In the Text Box Styles group, click **Change Shape**	To display the Change Shape gallery.
Under Flowchart, select as shown	
	To change the text box to a rounded rectangle. The shape is still fairly similar to the organization chart shapes, so you'll apply a style to change the shape and formatting.
5 In the Text Box Styles group, select a style of your choice	To apply the new style to the text box. The text might no longer fit in the text box.
6 Adjust the text box's height	(If necessary.) To fit the text.
7 Deselect all shapes	Click a blank area.
8 Update and close the document	

Topic C: Formatting text graphically

This topic covers the following Microsoft Certified Application Specialist exam objectives for Word 2007.

#	Objective
3.3.1	Insert and modify WordArt
3.3.2	Insert Pull Quotes
3.3.3	Insert and modify drop caps

Working with WordArt

Explanation

WordArt is a gallery of text styles you can use to create decorative effects in a document. To view this gallery, click WordArt, located in the Text group on the Insert tab. In the gallery, click a style to open the Edit WordArt Text dialog box, shown in Exhibit 6-7.

In the Edit WordArt Text dialog box, enter the text that you want to insert as WordArt in your document. You can also change the font and font size and apply bold or italic formatting.

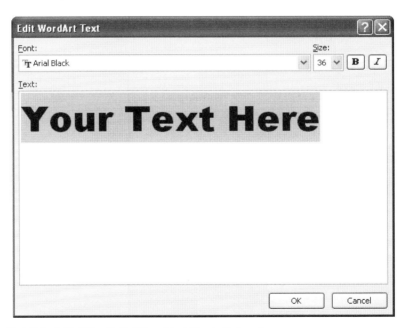

Exhibit 6-7: The Edit WordArt Text dialog box

When you select WordArt that has been inserted in a document, the WordArt Tools appear, adding a Format tab to the Ribbon. Using the tools on this tab, you can further modify the decorative text. You can change the spacing of the text, change the WordArt style, add or modify shadow effects, modify 3-D effects, and change the position of the text in the document, among other things.

C-1: Using WordArt

Here's how	Here's why
1 Open Announcement	From the current unit folder.
Save the document as **My announcement**	In the current unit folder.
2 Drag to select the first line of text	"A word from the chairman." (You can also triple-click in the line to select it.)
3 Activate the Insert tab	
In the Text group, click **WordArt**	To open the WordArt gallery.
4 Select the WordArt style of your choice	To open the Edit WordArt Text dialog box. The selected text, "A word from the chairman," appears in the dialog box as the text to be formatted.
Click **OK**	To close the dialog box and apply the WordArt style you selected to the selected text. The WordArt Tools appear, with the Format tab active.
5 In the WordArt Styles group, click as shown	(The Shape Fill button.) To open a gallery of color options.
Select the color of your choice	To change the color of the WordArt text.
6 In the WordArt Styles group, click as shown	(The Change WordArt Shape button.) To open a gallery of different WordArt shapes.
Select the shape of your choice	To adjust the overall shape of the WordArt text.

Using drop caps

Explanation

A *drop cap* is a large initial capital letter that extends below the first line of text in a paragraph. The drop cap adds visual interest and can be used to begin a document or a chapter, for example.

There are two variations of a drop cap: *dropped* and *in-margin*. Exhibit 6-8 shows an example of a dropped drop cap. The dropped letter is included within the document margins, along with the rest of the document text.

Exhibit 6-8: An example of a dropped drop cap

Exhibit 6-9 shows an example of an in-margin drop cap, which is placed in the document margin.

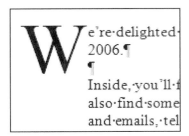

Exhibit 6-9: An example of an in-margin drop cap

To add a drop cap, place the insertion point in the paragraph that you want to begin with a drop cap. On the Insert tab, in the Text group, click Drop Cap and select the type of drop cap you prefer.

You can change the font of the drop-cap letter and change the distance of the text around it. To make such modifications, you select the drop cap, click Drop Cap in the Text group, and choose Drop Cap Options to open the Drop Cap dialog box. Make your changes and click OK.

C-2: Inserting and modifying a drop cap

Here's how	Here's why
1 Place the insertion point in the first paragraph of the document text	It begins with "We're delighted to present."
2 Activate the Insert tab	If necessary.
3 In the Text group, click **Drop Cap**	To display the Drop Cap gallery.
4 Point to Dropped	The size of the document's first letter, "W," is increased.
Point to In margin	The large "W" is placed in the margin of the document.
5 Choose **Dropped**	To create a drop cap.
6 In the Text group, click **Drop Cap**	
Choose **Drop Cap Options...**	To open the Drop Cap dialog box.
7 Observe the options	In addition to changing the position of the drop cap or removing it altogether, you can change its font and the distance of the text around it.
8 From the Font list, select a font	To assign a different font to the drop cap.
9 In the Lines to drop box, enter **5**	To increase the size of the capital letter to span five lines.
Click **OK**	To apply the changes.
10 Update the document	

Adding pull quotes to a document

Explanation

A *pull quote* is a brief phrase excerpted from body text. (It doesn't have to be an actual quotation.) This phrase or quote is typically enlarged or set apart from the body text by other formatting, as shown in Exhibit 6-10. You can use pull quotes to emphasize specific phrases or quotes and to add visual interest to a document.

You can use the Building Blocks Organizer to quickly insert pull quotes in a document. To do so:

1 Open the document that will contain the pull quote.
2 Activate the Insert tab. Click Quick Parts and choose Building Blocks Organizer.
3 From the Building blocks list, select the quote style you want to use.
4 Click Insert to add the formatted text box to your document.
5 In the text box, enter the desired phrase or quote.
6 Using the Text Box Tools | Format tab, you can change the appearance of the text box as desired.
7 Drag and resize the text box as needed.

Exhibit 6-10: An example of a pull quote

Do it!

C-3: Inserting a pull quote

Here's how	Here's why
1 Select the fourth body paragraph	It begins "We're sure you'll find enough here." You'll place this text in a pull quote.
Press CTRL + X	To cut the text from the document and place it on the Clipboard.
Press DELETE	To delete the extra blank line.
2 Activate the Insert tab	
3 Open the Building Blocks Organizer dialog box	In the Text group, click Quick Parts and choose Building Blocks Organizer.
From the Building blocks list, select **Braces Quote**	To identify the style of pull quote you'd like to use. Notice that this building block is located in the Text Boxes gallery.
Click **Insert**	To add the building block to the document.
4 Press CTRL + V	To insert your text inside the text box.
5 Drag the selection handles to resize the text box	We're·sure·you'll·find·enough·here· to·keep·you·cooking·for·some· time!¶
	(Your text box might appear slightly different depending on how you resize it.) To fit the text box more closely around the text.
6 Point near one of the braces, as shown	
	The mouse pointer changes its shape, so you can drag the entire text box.
Drag the text box to the lower-right corner of the document	To move the quote to a blank area of the document.
7 Activate the Format tab	(If necessary.) On the Text Box Tools tab.
8 Click **Shadow Effects**	(In the Shadow Effects group.) To display a gallery of shadow effects.
Under Drop Shadow, select Shadow Style 3	
	To add a drop shadow to the pull quote.

9 Click anywhere in the document   To deselect the text box and observe the document.

Update and close the document

Unit summary: Graphics

Topic A   In this topic, you used the **SmartArt** button to create an organization chart, and you used the SmartArt Tools tabs to modify the organization chart.

Topic B   In this topic, you created and modified a **shape**. You also inserted and formatted a **text box**. In addition, you learned how to arrange multiple objects by changing their **alignment** and **stacking order**. Finally, you changed an object's shape.

Topic C   In this topic, you used **WordArt** and **drop caps** to format text graphically. You also inserted a **pull quote** in a document. You learned that by making dramatic visual changes to text, you can add interest and visual appeal to a document.

Independent practice activity

In this activity, you'll create and format a process chart. You'll also insert and format a text box.

1   Create a new, blank document and save it as **My practice graphics** in the current unit folder.

2   Create a process chart that uses the Basic Process SmartArt graphic.

3   Name the diagram boxes **Meet new supplier**, **Examine products**, and **Finalize approval**.

4   Add a fourth box with the text **Follow up**, as shown in Exhibit 6-11. (*Hint*: In the Text pane, with the last text item selected, press Enter.)

5   Apply the Colorful Range – Accent Colors 3 to 4 color scheme. (*Hint*: Use the Change Colors button on the Design tab.)

6   Change the "Follow up" box to Orange, Accent 6, Darker 25%. (*Hint*: On the SmartArt Tools tab, activate the Format tab.)

7   Draw a text box above the "Examine products" box. (*Hint*: Use the Insert tab.)

8   In the text box, enter **Test all products we plan to purchase**.

9   Format the text as Trebuchet MS, 10 pt, centered.

10 Change the text box shape to the Down Arrow Callout shape, as shown in Exhibit 6-12. (*Hint*: This shape is located in the Block Arrows group. You can find it on the Text Box Tools tab; in the Text Box Styles group, use the Change Shape button.)

11 Resize and reposition the text box to display all the text, as shown in Exhibit 6-13.

12 Fill the text box with the color of your choice.

13 Update and close the document.

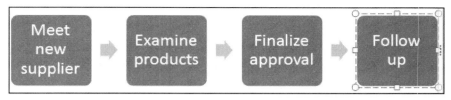

Exhibit 6-11: The process chart at the end of Step 4 in the independent practice activity

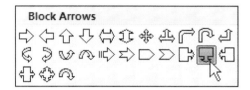

Exhibit 6-12: Selecting the new shape described in Step 10 in the independent practice activity

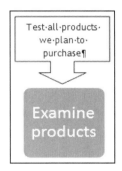

Exhibit 6-13: The final text box shape as it appears after Step 11 in the independent practice activity

Review questions

1 Which button on the Insert tab should you use to create a diagram?

   A Picture

   B SmartArt

   C Chart

   D Clip Art

2 How can you add text within a diagram?

   A Draw a text box over the diagram box.

   B On the Insert tab, click Insert Object and choose Object.

   C Right-click the box and choose Insert Text.

   D Enter text in the Text pane.

3 Which Ribbon tab should you use to change the color of a single box in a diagram?

   A Format

   B Layout

   C Home

   D Page Layout

4 How can you create a shape that contains text? (Choose all that apply.)

   A On the Insert tab, click Text Box and choose Draw Text Box.

   B Draw a shape, select it, activate the Drawing Tools | Format tab, and click Text Wrapping.

   C Draw a shape, select it, activate the Drawing Tools | Format tab, and click Add Text.

   D Draw a shape, select it, activate the Drawing Tools | Format tab, and click Edit Shape.

5 If a selected shape appears on top of another shape, where they overlap, how can you move the selected shape behind the other shape?

   A Activate the Drawing Tools | Format tab and click Change Shape.

   B Activate the Drawing Tools | Format tab and click Send to Back.

   C Activate the Drawing Tools | Format tab, click Align, and choose Align Top.

   D Activate the Drawing Tools | Format tab, click Align, and choose Align Bottom.

6 Where are the WordArt and Drop Cap tools located?

   A In the SmartArt Style group on the SmartTools | Format tab

   B In the Design group on the Page Layout tab

   C In the Text group on the Insert tab

   D In the Styles group on the WordArt Tools | Format tab

Unit 7

Managing document revisions

Unit time: 45 minutes

Complete this unit, and you'll know how to:

A Track changes while editing; review and accept revisions; view changes by different reviewers; restrict edits to tracked changes; and merge revisions.

B Insert, print, and delete comments.

Topic A: Tracking changes in a document

This topic covers the following Microsoft Certified Application Specialist exam objectives for Word 2007.

#	Objective
1.4.1	**Customize Word options** • Personalize username and initials
5.1.2	**Change window views** • Arrange all
5.2.1	**Compare document versions** • Manage multiple documents simultaneously
5.2.2	**Merge document versions** • Merge into new document
5.2.3	**Combine revisions from multiple authors**
5.3.1	**Display markup** • Display tracked changes and comments by reviewer
5.3.2	**Enable, disable, accept, and reject tracked changes** • Enable and disable track changes • Accept and reject changes
5.3.3	**Change tracking options** • Set reviewer options • Set balloon options • Modify insertions and deletions • Track formatting changes • Track moves
6.2.4	**Protect documents** • Set editing restrictions (This objective is also covered in the unit titled "Templates and building blocks" and in *Word 2007: Advanced*, in the unit titled "Forms.")

Enabling Track Changes

Explanation

Your document might go through a revision process, which might include you as well as other reviewers. If so, you can maintain a record of who makes which changes, and then you can choose to accept or reject each change. You can use the Track Changes feature to view changes and comments, and you can see changes made by specific reviewers. A *reviewer* is a person who evaluates a document and changes it.

To use the Track Changes feature, you must first turn it on. To do so, either activate the Review tab and click the Track Changes button in the Tracking group, or press Ctrl+Shift+E. Changes that you or another reviewer make will appear in different colors and can appear with different formatting. For example, you can choose to have deletions appear in red with bold formatting.

To modify the settings for Track Changes:

1 In the Tracking group, click Track Changes and choose Change Tracking Options to open the Track Changes Options dialog box, shown in Exhibit 7-1.

2 In the Markup section of this dialog box, specify the marks and colors that you want to use to indicate insertions, deletions, changed lines, and comments.

3 Click OK.

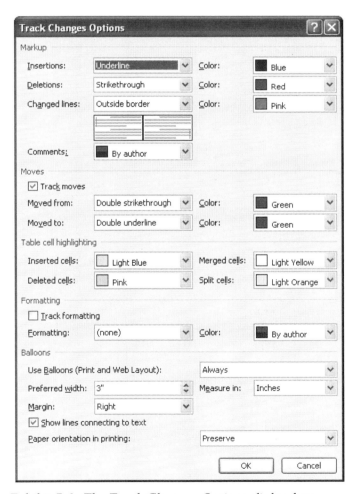

Exhibit 7-1: The Track Changes Options dialog box

When the document is in Draft or Outline view, markups appear directly in the text line. However, you can also view markups in Print Layout, Full Screen Reading, and Web Layout views. In these views, some markups appear in balloons (similar to callouts) in the margin, as shown in Exhibit 7-2. Use the Balloons section of the Track Changes Options dialog box to control the location and appearance of the balloons.

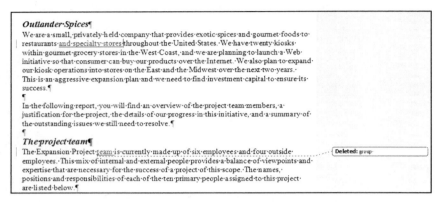

Exhibit 7-2: Tracked changes and a corresponding balloon in Print Layout view

Do it!   **A-1: Tracking changes while editing**

Here's how	Here's why
1 Open Roles	From the current unit folder.
Save the document as **My roles**	In the current unit folder.
2 Activate the Review tab	
In the Tracking group, click as shown	To display a menu.
Choose **Change Tracking Options...**	To open the Track Changes Options dialog box.
3 Under Markup, display the Insertions list	By default, inserted text is underlined. However, you can change the insertion indicator to be color only, bold, italic, double underline, or strikethrough.
Press (ESC)	To close the list without changing the selection.
From the Color list to the right of the Insertions list, select **Blue**	To change the color of all insertions to blue, instead of having a different color for each author's changes.
4 Display the Deletions list	By default, deleted text is indicated with strikethrough marks. You will set deletions to show up in red.
Press (ESC)	
5 From the Color list to the right of the Deletions list, select **Red**	You might need to scroll the list.
6 Set the Changed lines color to **Pink**	
7 Under Moves, observe the settings	By default, when you move text, it will be tracked. The original location will be denoted by a green strikethrough line. The destination will be denoted by a green double underline.
8 From the Use Balloons (Print and Web Layout) list, select **Always**	Located under Balloons, near the bottom of the dialog box.
Click **OK**	To save the markup settings and close the Track Changes Options dialog box.

9	In the Tracking group, click as shown	
		To enable change tracking. (If this feature is enabled, clicking the button again will disable change tracking.)
10	Switch to Draft view	Click the Draft button in the status bar.
	Verify that the document's magnification is 100%	The zoom level is displayed on the right side of the status bar.
11	Under "The project team," in the first line of the body paragraph, select **group**	*The·project·team*¶ The·Expansion·Project·group·is· employees.·This·mix·of·internal·
	Enter **team**	*The·project·team*¶ The·Expansion·Project·~~group~~·team·is· employees.·This·mix·of·internal·and·
		The inserted text is blue and underlined, while the deleted text is red and struck through. In addition, a pink vertical line on the left side of the page indicates a change.
12	In the first body paragraph, insert **and specialty stores**, as shown	*Outlander·Spices*¶ We·are·a·small,·privately·held·company·tha restaurants·<u>and·specialty·stores</u>·throughout· within·gourmet·grocery·stores·in·the·West·(
	Delete the text from **Kim Leong** to the end of the document, as shown	You might need to scroll to the bottom of the document.
	¶ ~~Kim·Leong,·Customer·Service·Representative~~¶ ~~Kim's·role·is·to·oversee·customer·service·support·to·new·and·current·customers.·He·will·~~ ~~monitor·the·demands·on·our·current·system·and·work·with·Elise·to·specify·upgrades·to·~~ ~~our·telephone·system.·Kim·also·will·play·an·integral·role·in·determining·the·requirements·~~ ~~of·the·online·ordering·system,·and·he·will·oversee·the·creation·of·a·training·initiative·and·~~ ~~documentation·for·the·new·system.~~¶	
13	Switch to Print Layout view	Click the Print Layout button in the status bar.
14	Update the document	

Reviewing revisions

Explanation

When someone else edits your work and returns it for your approval, you'll probably want to review the suggested changes. As you review the changes, you can either accept or reject them.

To accept a change, select it and click the Accept button on the Review tab. You can accept all of the changes at once by clicking Accept and choosing Accept All Changes in Document.

To reject a change, select it and click the Reject button on the Review tab. You can reject all changes at once by clicking Reject and choosing Reject All Changes in Document.

To find changes quickly, click Next or Previous in the Changes group on the Review tab.

Do it!

A-2: Reviewing and accepting revisions

Here's how	Here's why
1 Place the insertion point at the beginning of the document	(Press Ctrl+Home.) You'll review the revisions.
2 In the Changes group, click **Next**	To select the first change in the document—you inserted "and specialty stores."
In the Changes group, click as shown	
	To accept this change and move to the next one.
3 Click the upper part of the Accept button twice	To accept the change and move to the next one. Because you replaced text, there are actually two changes to review—the deletion of the original text, and the insertion of the new text—before moving on to the next change.
4 Click **Reject**	To reject the deletion of the text about Kim Leong. A message box states that there are no more comments or tracked changes in the document.
Click **OK**	To accept the message.
5 Verify that the text from "Kim Leong" to the end of the document is selected	
Press CTRL + X	To cut the text from the document and place it on the Clipboard.
6 Click to the left of "Aileen MacElvoy"	To move the insertion point.
Press CTRL + V	To move the text about Kim Leong to this location. In its new location, moved text appears in green with a double underline.
Press ↵ ENTER twice	To separate the two paragraphs, modifying the insertion. The change appears in blue.
7 Update and close the document	

Multiple reviewers

Explanation

You might want to view only the revisions or only the comments inserted in a document. To do so, activate the Review tab, click Show Markup in the Tracking group, and choose which elements to show or hide. For example, if you want to view only the comments, click the other options to deselect them—by default, all of the options are selected.

You can also view the changes made by a specific person. To do this, click Show Markup and choose Reviewers to display a menu with each reviewer's name, as shown in Exhibit 7-3. In the menu, All Reviewers is checked by default. To view only the changes made by a specific person, first deselect all reviewers by choosing All Reviewers; then choose the reviewer whose revisions or comments you want to see.

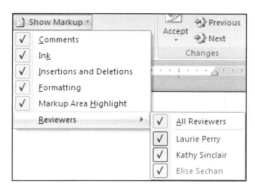

Exhibit 7-3: A list of reviewers for a document

Personalizing Word

To be identified by name as a reviewer, as shown in Exhibit 7-3, personalize your copy of Word. To do this:

1   Click the Office button and click Word Options to open the Word Options dialog box.

2   Verify that Popular is selected in the left pane.

3   Under "Personalize your copy of Microsoft Office," in the User name box, enter your name.

4   Click OK.

A-3: Viewing changes by different reviewers

Here's how	Here's why
1 Open Review	From the current unit folder.
Save the document as **My review**	In the current unit folder.
2 Activate the Review tab	
Ensure that Final Showing Markup appears in the Display for Review list, as shown	
Scroll in the document	To view the changes made by all of the reviewers. Three reviewers have each made a change.
3 Click **Show Markup**	In the Tracking group.
Choose **Reviewers, All Reviewers**	To clear the All Reviewers option, turning it off.
4 Click **Show Markup** and choose **Reviewers, Elise Sechan**	To show markups added by Elise Sechan.
Scroll in the document	To view only the changes made by Elise Sechan.
5 View Kathy Sinclair's changes	(Click Show Markup and choose Reviewers, Kathy Sinclair.) Both Elise Sechan's and Kathy Sinclair's changes are now displayed.
Click **Show Markup** and choose **Reviewers, Elise Sechan**	To display only Kathy Sinclair's changes.
6 Open the Word Options dialog box	Click the Office button and click Word Options.
Verify that Popular is selected in the left pane	
In the User name box, enter your name	To personalize Word.
In the Initials box, enter your initials	
Click **OK**	To accept these changes.

7	Enable Track Changes	Click the upper portion of the Track Changes button; or click the lower portion of the button and choose Track Changes.
8	Edit the document	Make any change you like.
9	Click **Show Markup** and choose **Reviewers**	Notice that your name appears in the list of document reviewers. This occurs because you personalized Word.
	Scroll in the document	To view both your changes and Kathy's changes.
10	Update and close the document	

Restricting edits

Explanation

If you want to protect a document from unwanted edits, you can restrict the edits to only tracked changes. In other words, any changes that someone makes will be recorded as tracked changes. Then, when the document is returned, you can decide whether to accept or reject the changes.

To restrict editing to tracked changes:

1 Open the Restrict Formatting and Editing pane.

2 Under Editing restrictions, check "Allow only this type of editing in the document."

3 From the list under Editing restrictions, select Tracked changes.

4 Under Start enforcement, click Yes, Start Enforcing Protection to open the Start Enforcing Protection dialog box.

5 In the "Enter new password (optional)" box, enter the password.

6 In the "Reenter password to confirm" box, enter the same password.

7 Click OK.

If you want to accept or reject the changes in a protected document, you first need to unprotect it.

Do it!

A-4: Restricting edits to tracked changes

Here's how	Here's why
1 Open Team	From the current unit folder.
Save the document as **My team**	In the current unit folder.
2 Open the Restrict Formatting and Editing pane	Activate the Review tab and click Protect Document.
3 Under Editing restrictions, check **Allow only this type of editing in the document**	You'll specify the type of editing restrictions.
From the list under Editing restrictions, select **Tracked changes**	To prevent other users from making untracked changes and from accepting or rejecting tracked changes. You'll be the only person who can accept or reject the changes in this document.

4 Under Start enforcement, click **Yes, Start Enforcing Protection**	To open the Start Enforcing Protection dialog box.
In the "Enter new password (optional)" box, enter **password**	Anyone who knows this password will be able to accept or reject the tracked changes.
In the "Reenter password to confirm" box, enter **password**	
Click **OK**	To close the Start Enforcing Protection dialog box and apply the password settings. The Restrict Formatting and Editing pane displays a message stating that the document is password-protected and all edits will be tracked.
5 Under "The project team," edit "outside employees" to read **external consultants**	In the first sentence of the first paragraph under "The project team."
6 Select **external**	(The word you just added.) To select the revision. The Accept and Reject buttons on the Ribbon are disabled. You're not allowed to accept or reject changes made in the document.
7 In the Restrict Formatting and Editing pane, click **Stop Protection**	
In the Password box, enter **password**	
Click **OK**	The Accept and Reject buttons on the Ribbon are enabled.
8 In the Changes group, click **Accept**, as shown	
	To display a menu.
Choose **Accept All Changes in Document**	
9 Close the Restrict Formatting and Editing pane	
Update and close the document	

Working with multiple documents at once

Explanation

If you want to work on multiple documents simultaneously, it's helpful to view them simultaneously. After you've opened all the documents you want to work with, activate the View tab and click Arrange All in the Window group.

If you have two documents open simultaneously, you can view them side by side. To do so, click View Side by Side in the Window group on the View tab. By default, the windows will scroll synchronously to help you compare their content.

Do it!

A-5: Managing multiple documents simultaneously

Here's how	Here's why
1 Open Comments	From the current unit folder.
2 Open My review	(From the current unit folder.) This was originally the same document as Comments, but has since undergone some changes.
3 Activate the View tab	
In the Window group, click **Arrange All**	To display all open documents simultaneously. The documents are arranged one above the other.
In the Window group, click **View Side by Side**	To display the documents side by side.
4 On the View tab, click the Window group	(In either window.) To view the options available in the group. When there's not enough space to display the Ribbon groups in their entirety, they're condensed into buttons.
Observe Synchronous Scrolling	This option is selected by default.
Click the Window group again	To close the group.
5 Scroll through either document	(Use both the horizontal and vertical scrollbars.) As you scroll in one document, the other document scrolls synchronously.
6 Close Comments	
Maximize Word	To maximize the remaining document window.

Merging revisions from two documents into a third document

Explanation

There might be times when several copies of the same document have been circulating for reviewers to mark up. Trying to combine all of the reviewers' marks into one document would be tedious. Instead, you can review the changes from two documents, decide which to keep, and then merge the two documents into a single document.

To merge two copies of a document in which changes have been tracked:

1   Activate the Review tab.
2   In the Compare group, click Compare and choose Combine to open the Combine Documents dialog box, shown in Exhibit 7-4.
3   From the Original document list, select the first marked-up document.
4   From the Revised document list, select the second marked-up document.
5   Click OK.

Note that in the previous steps, the merge uses the default settings. These include placing the merged results into a new, third document, which you can then name and save.

All tracked changes appear as marked revisions in the merged document, which appears in the Combined Document pane. The two original documents appear in the Original Document and Revised Document panes. In addition, a Summary pane provides a summary of all revisions in both documents. As in any other document, you can accept or reject each change.

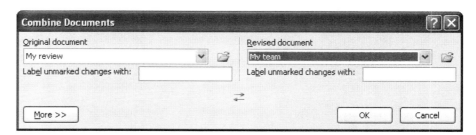

Exhibit 7-4: The Combine Documents dialog box

A-6: Merging revisions

Here's how	Here's why
1 Verify that My review is open	You'll merge changes from two documents into one final document that contains the changes from both.
Activate the Review tab	
2 In the Compare group, click **Compare**	
Choose **Combine...**	To open the Combine Documents dialog box.
3 From the Original document list, select **My review**	
From the Revised document list, select **My team**	These were originally the same document, but they now contain different changes.
Click **OK**	To open the documents. Several panes appear—the Summary pane, the Combined Document pane, the Original Document pane, and the Revised Document pane.
4 Scroll down in the Combined Document pane	To examine the changes. Both the Original Document and Revised Document panes scroll as well.
5 In the Combined Document pane, click **thirty**	(In the first paragraph.) To select the first change.
In the Changes group, click as shown and choose **Accept All Changes in Document**	
6 Update the document	Because you are saving the merged document, you need to enter a name.
Save the document as **My revisions**	In the current unit folder.
7 Close all documents and all panes	

Topic B: Working with comments

This topic covers the following Microsoft Certified Application Specialist exam objectives for Word 2007.

#	Objective
5.2.2	**Merge document versions** • Merge into existing document
5.4	**Insert, modify, and delete comments**

Inserting comments

Explanation

While reviewing a document, you might want to insert suggestions or comments. In Print Layout view, comments appear in balloons in the margin, as shown in Exhibit 7-5. Each comment appears with the initials of the person who made it (assuming that the initials were entered in the Set Up section of the Word Options dialog box).

To insert comments in a document:

1   Select the text that you want to comment on. This text will be highlighted after the comment is added.
2   On the Review tab, in the Comments group, click New Comment.
3   Type the comment.

To edit a comment you made, simply type in its comment balloon. You can also view and edit comments in the Reviewing pane. To open the Reviewing pane, click Reviewing Pane in the Tracking group.

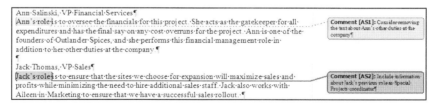

Exhibit 7-5: Comments in Print Layout view

B-1:   Inserting and modifying comments

Here's how	Here's why
1 Open Comments	From the current unit folder
Save the document as **My comments**	In the current unit folder.
2 In Ann Salinski's paragraph, select **Ann's role**	Ann·Salinski,·VP·Financial·Services¶ Ann's·role·is·to·oversee·the·financials expenditures·and·has·the·final·say·on·a
3 Activate the Review tab	
In the Comments group, click **New Comment**	A comment bubble appears to the right of the document.
4 Enter **Consider removing the text about Ann's other duties at the company**	
5 In the Tracking group, click **Reviewing Pane**	To show the comment in the Reviewing pane.
6 In the Reviewing pane, click at the end of the comment	To place the insertion point after the word "company" in the comment.
Press ⌨ SPACEBAR	
Enter **to streamline this document**	To provide additional commentary. Notice that the modification is reflected in the balloon.
In the Tracking group, click **Reviewing Pane** again	To hide the pane.
7 In Jack Thomas' paragraph, select **Jack's role**	You'll add a comment to this paragraph.
8 Add the comment **Include information about Jack's previous role as Special Projects director**	In the Comments group, click New Comment.
9 Update the document	

Merge changes and comments into an existing document

Explanation If you have two versions of a document and you want to insert one version's changes or comments into the other version, you can use the Combine Documents dialog box. To merge changes from one document into another:

1 On the Review tab, click Compare and choose Combine to open the Combine Documents dialog box.
2 From the Original document list, select the first copy of the document with comments or tracked changes (or both).
3 From the Revised document list, select the second copy of the reviewed document.
4 Click More to display additional options in the dialog box.
5 Under Comparison settings, check all items that you want Word to compare.
6 Under Show changes in, select either Original document or Revised document (to identify which document the combined results should be shown in).
7 Click OK.

Do it! ## B-2:   Merging changes into an existing document

Here's how	Here's why
1 Open the Combine Documents dialog box	On the Review tab, click Compare and choose Combine.
2 From the Original document list, select **My comments**	
3 From the Revised document list, select **Browse...**	The Open dialog box appears.
Select **My revisions**	When you combine both documents' comments, you'll have them added to this document.
Click **Open**	
4 Click **More**	To expand the Combine Documents dialog box so it displays additional options.
5 Under Comparison settings, clear all boxes except Comments	The only information you want to combine is the comments.
Under Show changes in, select **Revised document**	To show the combined comments in the revised document (My revisions).
Click **OK**	To add the comments from My comments to My revisions.
6 Update and close My revisions	

Printing document comments

You can print comments along with the comment text and number. To do so:

1 Click the Office button and choose Print to open the Print dialog box.
2 From the Print what list, select Document showing markup.
3 Click OK.

B-3:   Printing comments

Here's how	Here's why
1 Click	
Choose **Print**, **Print Preview**	To examine a preview of the printed page.
2 On the Print Preview tab, click **Print**	To open the Print dialog box.
In the Print what list, verify that Document showing markup is selected	You can also select List of markup from the list to print only the markup.
3 Click **OK**	(Click Cancel if you don't want to print at this time.) To print the document with comments.
Click **Close Print Preview**	(If necessary.) To return to Print Layout view.

Deleting comments

Explanation

You might want to delete some comments from a reviewed document. To do so, first place the insertion point either in the comment balloon or in the text to which the comment was added. Then, in the Comments group, click Delete.

Do it!

B-4: Deleting a comment

Here's how	Here's why
1 Place the insertion point within **Ann's role**	You'll delete the comment for this text.
2 In the Comments group, click **Delete**	To delete the comment.
3 Update and close the document	

Unit summary: Managing document revisions

Topic A   In this topic, you learned how to enable Word's **Track Changes** feature and change its settings. You also learned how to review and accept revisions, view changes made by different reviewers, and **restrict edits** to tracked changes. Finally, you learned how to **merge revisions** from two documents into one.

Topic B   In this topic, you learned how to insert, merge, print, and delete **comments**.

Independent practice activity

In this activity, you'll enable Track Changes to record the revisions you make in a document. Then you'll compare your revisions with those of another reviewer and combine them into one document.

1 Open Revisions practice (from the current unit folder), and save the document as **My revisions practice**.

2 Enable Track Changes.

3 On page 2, edit the heading "Healing benefits of herbs" to read **Health benefits of herbs**.

4 Accept all the changes in the document.

5 Add this comment to the last line of the document: **Add a topic on commonly used herbs and spices**.

6 Update and close the document.

7 Compare the revisions in the documents My revisions practice and Second reviewer (in the current unit folder).

8 Scroll in the Combined Document pane to see the revisions from each reviewer.

9 Accept all changes in the combined document.

10 Save the document as **My combined revisions** and close it.

11 Close all open documents and panes.

Review questions

1 How do you turn on the Track Changes feature?

2 In Print Layout view, with Track Changes turned on, where do deletions appear?

3 You want to send your document out for review, and you want to ensure that all edits are recorded as tracked changes. What should you do?

4 If you're viewing a document that contains comments in Draft view, how can you read the comments?

5 How do you print comments along with a document?

Unit 8

Web features

Unit time: 45 minutes

Complete this unit, and you'll know how to:

A Preview a document as a Web page, save a document as a Web page, open an HTML document in a browser, and edit an HTML document in Word.

B Insert a hyperlink in a document, navigate by using hyperlinks, and link to another document by using hyperlinks.

Topic A: Web pages

Explanation

Web pages are built using *Hypertext Markup Language,* or *HTML,* which is a standard markup language that allows you to display text, images, and multimedia files on the Web. Even if you're not familiar with HTML, you can create a Web page in Word by saving a document as a Web page. You can also use Word to open and edit Web pages, and you can send Word documents through e-mail.

Web Layout view

While creating a Web page in Word, you might want to see how the document will look when viewed online. To do this, you can use Web Layout view.

To switch to Web Layout view, do either of the following:

- On the View tab, in the Document Views group, click Web Layout.
- Click the Web Layout button on the right side of the status bar.

Sending documents via e-mail

As you work in Word and other Office programs, you might want to send a document you've created to another person via e-mail. Depending on the e-mail program you're using, the e-mail features and options might vary. When you attach a Word 2007 document, the recipient must have Word 2007 to view the attachment. If the recipient can't view the attachment, you can save the file as a Word 97-2003 document.

To send a Word document via e-mail:

1 Open the document you want to send.
2 Click the Office button and choose Send, Email. A new message opens in your default e-mail program, with the document attached.
3 Enter or select the recipient's e-mail address, and enter any message you want to include.
4 Click Send.

Do it!

A-1: Previewing a document as a Web page

Here's how	Here's why
1 Open About us	From the current unit folder.
2 Click as shown	
	(The Web Layout button, on the right side of the status bar.) To display the document in Web Layout view. The document now appears as it would in a browser window.
3 Scroll through the document	Notice that there are no page breaks in Web Layout view, and the margins are optimized for online viewing.

Saving documents as Web pages

Explanation

You save a Word document as a Web page by clicking the Office button and choosing Save As. In the Save As dialog box, select Web Page from the Save as type list. The file will be saved as an HTML document with the extension .htm, and all the graphics and images in the document will be saved in an associated folder. If you upload the Web page to a server, remember to include the folder containing the images for your page.

Changing the page title

The title bar of a Web page usually contains text called a *page title*, as shown in Exhibit 8-1. The title does not need to be long, but it should be descriptive.

To enter a new page title:

1 Click the Office button and choose Save As.
2 In the Save As dialog box, click Change Title to open the Set Page Title dialog box.
3 Enter a descriptive title and click OK.
4 Verify that the file name is correct, and verify that Web Page is selected in the Save as type list.
5 Click Save.

Exhibit 8-1: A title bar as displayed in a Web browser

Setting Web options

The Web Options dialog box, shown in Exhibit 8-2, contains a variety of settings you can use to tailor a document to your Web audience. For example, you can disable features that are not supported by certain browsers. To do so, activate the Browsers tab and select a category of Web browsers. (Keep in mind that most people won't be using the latest versions.) Then check "Disable features not supported by these browsers" and click OK.

To open the Web Options dialog box, click the Tools button in the Save As dialog box and choose Web Options.

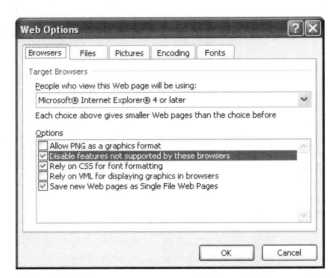

Exhibit 8-2: The Browsers tab of the Web Options dialog box

Do it!

A-2:   Saving a document as a Web page

Here's how	Here's why
1 Open the Save As dialog box	Click the Office button and choose Save As.
2 Edit the File name box to read **My web page**	
3 From the Save as type list, select **Web Page**	To save the document as a Web-page file with the .htm extension.
4 Click **Change Title**	(The Change Title button is below the Save as type list.) To open the Set Page Title dialog box.
Edit the Page title box to read **About Outlander Spices**	The title will appear in the browser's title bar when this Web page is displayed.
Click **OK**	To close the dialog box. The title appears below the Save as type list.
5 Click **Save**	To save the document and close the Save As dialog box.
6 Close the document	
7 Open Windows Explorer	
Navigate to the current unit folder	
Observe the contents of the folder My web page_files	This folder contains image files and XML files used to display the HTML document. These files would need to accompany the Web page if you were to upload it to a server.
Close Windows Explorer	

Opening HTML documents in a browser

Explanation

A *Web browser* is software used to access Web sites, which contain Web pages. One of the most commonly used Web browsers is Internet Explorer, although many other browsers exist.

To open an HTML document in Internet Explorer:

1 Click Start and choose All Programs, Internet Explorer. (You can also double-click the Internet Explorer icon on the desktop.)

2 Choose File, Open; browse to and select the desired file; and click Open.

3 Click OK.

You can also open a file in a browser by typing or pasting the Web page's address in the browser's Address box and pressing Enter.

Do it!

A-3: Opening an HTML document in a browser

Here's how	Here's why
1 Click **Start** and choose **All Programs, Internet Explorer**	
2 Select the contents of the Address box	(In the upper-left area of the browser window.) You'll open the file from within Internet Explorer.
In the Address box, type **C:\Student Data\Unit_XX\My web page.htm**	Where XX is the unit number.
Press ⏎ ENTER	To open the file in the browser window. The Web page resembles the way it looked in Web Page Preview in Word.
3 Observe the page title	It displays the text you entered in the Page title box: "About Outlander Spices."
4 Return to Word	Click the My web page button in the Windows taskbar.

Opening HTML documents for editing in Word

Explanation

When you need to edit an HTML document, you can do that in Word. To do so, open the HTML file in Word, as you would open a Word document. Then modify the document as necessary, and save the file; it will automatically be resaved as an HTML document.

If you're using Internet Explorer, you can also browse to a Web site and then choose File, Edit with Microsoft Office Word from the browser window. The file will be opened in Word, where you can edit it; however, it might not look the same as it does in the browser.

Do it!

A-4: Editing an HTML document in Word

Here's how	Here's why
1 In Word, open My web page	This is the Word document you saved as a Web page.
2 Place the insertion point as shown	All·spiced·up¶ |Outlander·Spices·opened world·and·select·gourmet You'll edit the document.
Enter **Welcome to Outlander Spices!**	
Press (SPACEBAR)	
3 Update the document	The document will automatically be saved as an HTML document.
4 View the Internet Explorer window	Click the Internet Explorer button in the Windows taskbar.
Press (F5)	To refresh the page. The updated version of the document is displayed.
Close Internet Explorer	(Click the Close button in the upper-right corner of the window.) To return to Word.

Topic B: Hyperlinks

This topic covers the following Microsoft Certified Application Specialist exam objective for Word 2007.

#	Objective
1.3.4	**Insert document navigation tools**
	• Hyperlinks

Inserting hyperlinks

Explanation

A *hyperlink*, or *link* for short, is text or an image that, when clicked, connects to another page, another location on the same page, another site, or some other resource. When you point to a hyperlink in Word, a ScreenTip appears. By default, hyperlinks are blue and underlined; however, some Web pages contain formatting that changes the default appearance of hyperlinks.

In Word, you can use hyperlinks to link to a Web page, to another document, or to another place in the same document. You can also use hyperlinks to create a new document or to send an e-mail message. To link to another place in the same document, it must have text formatted with outline levels.

To insert a hyperlink in a document:

1 Select the text that you want to make a hyperlink.

2 Open the Insert Hyperlink dialog box, shown in Exhibit 8-3. (You can press Ctrl+K or click the Hyperlink button on the Insert tab on the Ribbon.)

3 To specify a ScreenTip for the hyperlink, click ScreenTip, enter the desired text, and click OK.

4 In the Address box, enter the location of the HTML file, Word document, or other file to which you want to link.

5 Click OK.

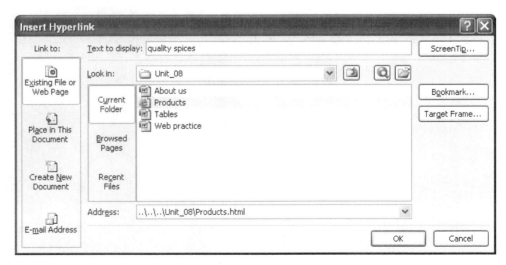

Exhibit 8-3: The Insert Hyperlink dialog box

Do it!

B-1: Inserting a hyperlink to an HTML file

Here's how	Here's why
1 Maximize Word	If necessary.
2 In the first paragraph, select **quality spices**	(In the third sentence.) You'll make this text a hyperlink.
Right-click the text	To display the shortcut menu.
Choose **Hyperlink...**	To open the Insert Hyperlink dialog box.
3 Click **ScreenTip**	To open the Set Hyperlink ScreenTip dialog box. You'll create a custom ScreenTip for your hyperlink to provide users with more information.
In the ScreenTip box, enter **Click to learn more about our products**	
Click **OK**	To close the dialog box.
4 Navigate to the current unit folder and select **Products**	This is an HTML file containing product information.
Click **OK**	To create the hyperlink. The text "quality spices" is formatted to indicate that it's a hyperlink.
5 Update the document	

Using hyperlinks

Explanation

In a Web browser, you simply click a hyperlink to navigate to its associated content. To use a hyperlink in Word, however, you press and hold Ctrl, and then click the hyperlink. When you click a hyperlink, the mouse pointer must be in the shape of a pointing finger.

If a hyperlink points to a file, the linked file will open in its source program. After you click a hyperlink, its color typically changes to indicate that it has been clicked. This is known as a *followed hyperlink.* You can change the default colors of hyperlinks and followed hyperlinks by using the Manage Styles dialog box.

Do it!

B-2: Navigating with hyperlinks

Here's how	Here's why
1 Point to the hyperlink	All-spiced up *Click to learn more about our products* *CTRL + click to follow link* Welcome to C open quality spices from all over the world and select gourm companies to have our own Web site. Customers from
	Word displays the custom ScreenTip you created, plus a message on how to follow the link.
2 Press and hold CTRL	All-spiced up *Click to learn more about our products* *CTRL + click to follow link* Welcome to C open quality spices from all over the world and select gourm compan to have our own Web site. Customers from
	The pointer changes to a pointing finger, indicating that this is a hyperlink.
Click the hyperlink	To open the product information in Internet Explorer.
Release CTRL	
3 Click as shown	C:\Student Data Outlander Spices
	(The Back button is on the Browser toolbar.) To go back to the Word document. The hyperlink changes color, indicating that you've followed the link.

Linking to other types of files

Explanation

In addition to linking to Web pages, you can link to other types of files, such as Word or Excel files. For example, you might want to open a Word document that relates to some text in your current document, or you might want to open an Excel spreadsheet. To do this, you can create a hyperlink in the same way you would if you were linking to an HTML file.

Do it!

B-3:   Creating a hyperlink to a Word document

Here's how	Here's why
1 Under the heading Expansion project, select **kiosk operations**	You'll make this text a hyperlink to another Word document.
Open the Insert Hyperlink dialog box	Press Ctrl+K.
Select **Tables**	From the current unit folder.
Click **OK**	To close the dialog box.
2 Observe the hyperlink ScreenTip	(Point to the link.) The default ScreenTip displays the file name and path of the linked file.
3 Press (CTRL) and click the hyperlink	To open the Tables document in Word.
Close the document	
4 Update and close My web page	

Unit summary: Web features

Topic A   In this topic, you examined a document in Web Layout view. You also saved a document as a **Web page** and then opened it in a browser. Finally, you learned how to edit an HTML document in Word.

Topic B   In this topic, you inserted a **hyperlink** to an HTML file, and you learned how to navigate by using hyperlinks. You also created a hyperlink that links to another Word document.

Independent practice activity

In this activity, you'll open a document and save it as a Web page. Then you'll insert a hyperlink that points to an HMTL file you created previously.

1 Open Web practice (from the current unit folder), and save it as **My web practice**.

2 Preview the document as a Web page by using Web Layout view.

3 Save the file as a Web page named **My practice page**, and change the page title to **The Outlander Spices Team**.

4 Open My practice page in Internet Explorer.

5 Close Internet Explorer.

6 In the first body paragraph, make the text **privately held company** a hyperlink to the file **My web page** (in the current unit folder).

7 Use the hyperlink to display the HTML file.

8 Close Internet Explorer and return to Word.

9 Update and close the document.

10 Close Word. If prompted, **don't** save changes to Building Blocks.

Review questions

1 What is the command to send a Word document as an e-mail attachment?

2 How can you check the appearance of your Web page before you save or publish it?

3 You want a title to appear in the browser's title bar when your Web page is opened. How do you edit a Web page's title in Word?

4 Describe the steps for inserting a hyperlink in a document.

5 You can use a hyperlink to link to all of the following except:

   A An Excel spreadsheet

   B Another Word document

   C A Word document located on someone else's computer

   D A Web page

Course summary

This summary contains information to help you bring the course to a successful conclusion. Using this information, you will be able to:

A Use the summary text to reinforce what you've learned in class.

B Determine the next courses in this series (if any), as well as any other resources that might help you continue to learn about Word 2007.

Topic A: Course summary

Use the following summary text to reinforce what you've learned in class.

Unit summaries

Unit 1

In this unit, you learned how to examine text formatting and compare the formatting of two selections by using the **Reveal Formatting** pane. Then you applied a **style**, created a paragraph style by example, based one style on another, and created a character style. You also modified a style by using the **Manage Styles** dialog box, overrode a style, modified the Normal style, and **exported** a style. Next, you created an **outline** and learned how to organize and format outlines. Finally, you viewed a document and navigated through it by using the **Document Map** and **Thumbnails** panes.

Unit 2

In this unit, you learned how to insert and delete **section breaks**. Then you formatted pages in a section. Next, you inserted section headers and footers and formatted section page numbers. You also formatted text into **columns**, inserted column breaks, and added a heading that spans columns.

Unit 3

In this unit, you **aligned text** in a table and changed the orientation of text in a cell. You also **merged** and **split** table cells and resized rows. Next, you changed a table's **borders** and applied **shading** to cells. Then you **sorted data** in a table. You also split a table, repeated a **header row** on multiple pages, and entered **formulas** in a table. Finally, you applied and modified **table styles**.

Unit 4

In this unit, you prepared and printed an address on every label on a sheet of **labels**. You also prepared and printed an address on a single **envelope**.

Unit 5

In this unit, you created a document from a **template**. Then you saved and used your own template, and you used the Templates folder to store a custom template. You also used the **Building Blocks Organizer** to insert a sidebar and header in a document. Next, you created, modified, and deleted your own building blocks. In addition, you **protected** a document with a password. Then you viewed and edited document **properties**, and you viewed a document's **statistics**.

Unit 6

In this unit, you created and modified an **organization chart**. You also created and modified a **shape**, and you inserted and formatted a **text box**. Next, you arranged multiple objects by adjusting their **alignment** and **stacking order**. You also changed an object's shape. Finally, you formatted text graphically by using WordArt, drop caps, and pull quotes.

Unit 7

In this unit, you enabled and changed settings for Word's **Track Changes** feature. You also learned how to review and accept revisions, view changes made by different reviewers, and **restrict edits** to tracked changes. Next, you **merged revisions** from two documents into one. Finally, you learned how to insert, print, and delete **comments**.

Unit 8

In this unit, you learned how to **preview** a document as a **Web page**. You also saved a document as a Web page and then opened it in a browser, and you learned how to edit an HTML document in Word. Finally, you inserted **hyperlinks** and learned how to navigate by using hyperlinks.

Topic B: Continued learning after class

It is impossible to learn to use any software effectively in a single day. To get the most out of this class, you should begin working with Word 2007 to perform real tasks as soon as possible. We also offer resources for continued learning.

Next courses in this series

This is the second course in this series. The next courses are:

- *Word 2007: Advanced*
  - Merge a recipient list with a form letter
  - Insert and modify objects
  - Use watermarks and themes
  - Create and protect forms
  - Use macros to automate tasks
  - Customize the Quick Access toolbar
  - Create a master document
  - Create an XML document
- *Word 2007: VBA Programming*
  - Build applications
  - Debug code
  - Automate data entry
  - Merge data files
  - Create forms
  - Build tables
  - Secure information
  - Share data

Other resources

For more information, visit www.axzopress.com.

Word 2007: Intermediate

Quick reference

Button	Shortcut keys	Function
		Displays a list of commonly used file-related commands, such as Open, Save As, and Print.
	SHIFT + F1	Opens the Reveal Formatting task pane.
Track Changes	CTRL + SHIFT + E	Turns Track Changes on or off.
Hyperlink	CTRL + K	Opens the Insert Hyperlink dialog box.
		Clears the formatting from selected text.
		Opens the Create New Style from Formatting dialog box.
		Opens the Manage Styles dialog box.
		Promotes the selected text to the Heading 1 style in an outline.
	ALT + SHIFT + ←	Promotes the selected text to the next highest outline level.
	ALT + SHIFT + →	Demotes the selected text to the next lowest outline level.
		Demotes the selected text to Body text outline level.
	ALT + SHIFT + ↑	Moves the selected paragraph up in the outline, without changing its outline level.
	ALT + SHIFT + ↓	Moves the selected paragraph down in the outline, without changing its outline level.
	ALT + SHIFT + +	If collapsed, expands the selected outline level.

Button	Shortcut keys	Function
	ALT + SHIFT + _	If expanded, collapses the selected outline level.
		In a header or footer, removes the link to the previous section.
		Moves to the previous header or footer.
		Opens a document in your default Web browser.

Glossary

Adjustment handle

A yellow diamond that appears if you can adjust a selected shape. You can drag an adjustment handle to reshape a drawn object.

Callout

A shape used for labeling pictures or other graphics.

Column break

A mark that indicates the end of a column.

Comment

A note or suggestion that is attached to selected text. In Print Layout view, comments appear as balloons in the margins.

Continuous section break

A break that starts a new section on the same page.

Document Map

A window that displays document headings by outline level.

Drawing canvas

A space where you can work on graphics or drawings in Word.

Editing restrictions

A Word feature that enables you to protect a document by selecting the kind of editing allowed in it: Tracked Changes, Comments, Filling in forms, or No changes (Read only).

Even Page section break

A break that starts a new section on the next even-numbered page.

Field

A placeholder for data that can change, such as the current date and time.

Followed hyperlink

A link that has been used. Its color typically changes to indicate its status as a followed link.

Formatting restrictions

A Word feature that enables you to protect a document by preventing unauthorized users from modifying or using styles that you specify.

Formula

A mathematical statement used to perform arithmetic operations, such as calculating an average or a sum.

Function

A built-in formula used to perform calculations. For example, the SUM function adds the numbers in selected cells.

Header row

The first row in a table, typically containing descriptive headings for the data in each column.

Hyperlink

Text or an image that, when clicked, connects to another page, another location on the same page, another site, or some other resource.

Hypertext Markup Language (HTML)

A standard markup language that allows you to display text, images, and multimedia files on the Web.

Markup

In Word, the marks and colors that indicate insertions, deletions, formatting changes, and changed lines when Track Changes is used.

Merging cells

The combining of two or more cells in the same row or column to form a single cell.

Next Page section break

A break that starts a new section on the next page.

Odd Page section break

A break that starts a new section on the next odd-numbered page.

Outline

A way of showing the structure of a document by displaying its headings and subheadings (if they're assigned an outline level).

Outline view

A Word view that enables you to collapse and expand text located under headings to view different levels of detail.

Page title

Text that describes a Web page and that is displayed in the title bar of a browser.

Reviewer

A person who evaluates a document and changes it or comments on it.

Rotate handle

The green circle that appears near the top of a selected shape and is used to turn, or rotate, the shape.

Section

A portion of a document in which you can set certain formatting options—such as margins, headers and footers, page numbering, and page orientation—separately from the rest of the document.

Sizing handles

White circles that appear at each corner and along each edge of an imaginary rectangle, indicating the boundary of a selected shape.

Splitting cells

The process of dividing a cell into two or more cells.

Stacking order

The order in which objects overlap.

Style

A named set of formatting options, used to define the appearance of recurring text elements, such as headings or body text.

Template

A pre-designed document that contains formatting and boilerplate text or placeholder text. It provides the basis for quickly creating commonly used documents.

Text box

A drawn object in which you can enter text. Text boxes can be placed anywhere in a document.

Thumbnails

Miniature images of the pages in a document. Can be used to navigate through a large document in Word.

Web browser

Software used to access and view Web sites.

Index